C000234611

ANTA

THE FALKLANDS & SOUTH GEORGIA

Cadogan Books plc
27–29 Berwick Street, London W1V 3RF, UK
guides@cadogan.demon.co.uk

Distributed in North America by The Globe Pequot Press
6 Business Park Road, PO Box 833, Old Saybrook,
Connecticut 06475–0833

Copyright © Sara Wheeler 1997
Black and white illustrations © Suzan Kentli 1997

Book and cover design by Animage
Maps © Cadogan Guides, drawn by Map Creation Ltd

Series Editor: Rachel Fielding

Editing and proofreading: Linda McQueen
Indexing: Judith Wardman
Production: Book Production Services

A catalogue record for this book is available from the British Library
ISBN 1–86011–047–9

Please help us to keep this guide up to date

We have done our best to ensure that the information in this guide is correct at the time of going to press, but we would be delighted to receive any comments concerning existing entries or omissions, and to hear about your own experiences of Antarctica.

All contributors will be acknowledged in the next edition, and the best letters will receive a copy of the Cadogan Guide of their choice.

The author and publishers have made every effort to ensure the accuracy of the information in this book at the time of going to press. However, they cannot accept any responsibility for any loss, injury or inconvenience resulting from the use of information contained in this guide.

Printed and bound in Great Britain by Biddles Ltd

About the Author

Sara Wheeler is a London-based travel writer and broadcaster. *Terra Incognita*, the story of her seven-month journey through Antarctica, was published in 1996 to widespread acclaim. She is a qualified scuba diver and belly dancer, and has written three other books. She is currently co-editing an anthology of women's travel writing.

Picture Credits

All photographs used to illustrate this guide are by Sara Wheeler except the following:

Wildlife

From the **Bruce Coleman Collection**: *p.91*, gentoo penguin, Dr Eckart Pott; *p.92*, rockhopper penguins, Allan G. Potts; *p.92*, macaroni penguin, Mr Johnny Johnson; *p.92*, chinstrap penguin, Francisco Erize; *p.94*, elephant seal, Gordon Langsbury; *p.94*, crabeater seal, Francisco Erize; *p.96*, wandering albatross, Rinie Van Meurs; *p.97*, southern giant petrel, Dr Eckart Pott; *p.97*, grey-backed storm petrel, Rinie Van Meurs; *p.98*, blue-eyed shag and chicks, Leonard Lee Rue; *p.100*, southern minke whale, Bill Wood; *p.101*, killer whale, Jeff Foot.

History

From the **Royal Geographical Society**, London: *after p.138*, Scott's team and Scott, and *before p.139*, *Nimrod* party and *Endurance*.

Cover

The cover illustrations are based on photographs by Paul Findlay.

Contents

These things are not earthly, this is heaven.

Frank Hurley, Shackleton's photographer
on the 1914–17 Transantarctic Expedition

ICE CAVES

Introduction

Ever since the Ancient Greeks sensed that it was there, Antarctica has wielded a mysteriously poetic power over the human imagination. Pristine, invincible and supremely magnificent, it seems a symbol of innocence and purity, a world away from the urban chaos of the developed world.

If Antarctica exists so vividly in the mind, why is it that people are impelled to go there? What motivates men to travel to such a relentlessly inhospitable corner of the globe, a continent where a temperature of minus thirty degrees Celsius isn't especially cold and a ten-day whiteout is to be expected? In the early days of exploration they were spurred on by the quest for knowledge, a natural human impulse, or the hope of financial gain. But now? For the adventurers who tow their own sledges the continent represents a physical and psychological testing-ground, a chance to do something great—even the arena to pull off a stunt. For scientists it offers unique opportunities to unlock some of the remaining mysteries of Planet Earth, often by reaching back, far into geological time. And for the support staff who look after scientific logistics Antarctica is a unique working environment, a paid job without the nine-to-five.

For all these people, and for every tourist on a cruise ship, Antarctica also offers the most beautiful scenery in the world. That is my opinion, and I've travelled a bit.

Being in Antarctica has often enabled people to reach out towards the spiritual plane of their own existence. This was my experience. After spending seven months in Antarctica, much of it in a tent, I went home with a sense that I had realigned the focus of my life. Being in such a vast and unowned space, a whole continent without traffic jams and electricity bills, I had seen that the human spirit has a place in the natural order of things. I cannot explain exactly what that means, as it is a conviction that goes beyond words; but Antarctica taught me another way of looking at the world.

I remember looking up from a small camp in the lee of Mount Erebus and watching a turban of cloud dissolve over the summit. Antarctic light has a particular luminous quality, and that morning it seemed to be pouring down the treacherous slopes of the volcano and engulfing our camp in buttery sunshine. The ice underfoot was softly yielding, and I could see the Transantarctic mountains five miles away as if they were close to hand, each face coated in a purply glaze. The scene was immersed in quietness. It is impossible, I think, to convey the quality of Antarctic silence. The best description I have read comes from the work of the American novelist Jack London.

> Nature has many tricks wherewith she convinces man of his finity...but the most tremendous, the most stupefying of all, is the passive phase of the White Silence. All movement ceases, the sky clears, the heavens are as brass...[man] trembles at his audacity, realizes that his is a maggot's life, nothing more. Strange thoughts arise unsummoned, and the mystery of all things strive for utterance. And the fear of death, of God, of the universe, comes over him...it is then, if ever, man walks alone with God.

Away from the din of my life at home, I was soon surprised at what began to capture my imagination. I had never been very interested in birds, but as soon as I got to the Southern Ocean I was gripped. I spent many hours watching snow petrels glide across the cobalt blue. Apsley Cherry-Garrard wrote about these birds in my favourite polar book, *The Worst Journey in the World*. Cherry, as he was known, was the youngest of Captain Scott's men on the latter's second and tragic expedition.

> *There are many other beautiful sea-birds, but most beautiful of all are the Snowy petrels, which approach nearer to the fairies than anything else on earth. They are quite white, and seemingly transparent. They are the familiar spirits of the pack, which, except to nest, they seldom if ever leave, flying here and there independently in a mazy fashion, glittering against the blue sky like so many white moths, or shining snowflakes.*

I still find it extraordinary that a century ago the motor car had been invented but Antarctica had never heard a human voice. The best and the worst of what we can be is encapsulated in that short subsequent period when men came and gave Antarctica a history.

Most people are familiar with the bones of the Scott story—how he reached the South Pole five weeks after the Norwegian Roald Amundsen, and how the shock of discovering that he had been beaten nearly killed his spirit. Few know that Amundsen left a note for Scott in a little tent at the South Pole. The Norwegian party had named their camp at the Pole 'Polheim'. Amundsen's note said,

> *15 December 1911, Polheim*
>
> *Dear Captain Scott,*
>
> *As you are probably the first to reach this area after us I will ask you kindly to forward this letter to King Haakon VII. If you can use any of the articles left in this tent please do not hesitate to do so. The sledge left outside may be of use to you. With best regards I wish you safe return.*
>
> *Yours truly*
>
> *Roald Amundsen*

I believe that Antarctica has something to teach us all. The lucky few who can see it for themselves will know what I mean as soon as the first iceberg hoves into view. And those who don't travel south—I think they see their own icebergs, only in other ways.

Acknowledgements

The author would like to thank Guy Guthridge and his colleagues at the Office of Polar Programs in Virginia. The OPP, which is part of the National Science Foundation, administers the American Antarctic Program. Sara Wheeler also wishes to thank Frank Curry at the British Antarctic Survey in Cambridge, Mario Zuccelli and his team at the Italian Antarctic Programme, based in Rome, and the New Zealanders in Christchurch who send Kiwis south to Scott Base each year. All these people contributed vastly with logistical support and helpful advice.

Bob Headland, Archivist at the Scott Polar Research Institute, is an Antarctic wizard, and he scrutinised the manuscript before it went to press and gave us the benefit of his encyclopaedic knowledge. Writers on Antarctica tremble at this man's approach. Heartfelt thanks.

Finally, thanks to Rachel Fielding and Linda McQueen at Cadogan, and to Bill Colegrave for having a good idea.

Travel

As many as 10,000 tourists visit Antarctica each year, an acceleration rate of 0–10,000 in fewer than thirty years. Even as recently as 1991, the figure was 3000.

If your time is at a premium and you are content to see the Great White South from the air, you can take a Qantas daytrip over Antarctica from Australia. If on the other hand you have endless time and a taste for gambling you can hang around in Punta Arenas or Ushuaia and try to hitch a lift, for a modest daily sum, on a Chilean or Argentinian naval ship going to the South Shetlands, off the tip of the Antarctic Peninsula. If you are very lucky, you might even pick up a budget cruise from one of these ports. Alternatively, if you are an experienced sailor with lots of time and money you can try taking your own yacht south—it has been done. Or with twenty to thirty thousand US dollars you can fly to the Pole with a specialist expedition airline.

But if, like most people, none of the above suits your needs or budget, you will have to take a cruise.

Cruising to Antarctica

This is a recent phenomenon, but an increasingly popular one which looks set to become an entrenched feature on the cruise circuit. The only problem, of course, is that one is obliged to spend a long time aboard getting to the destination, with a limited amount to see *en route* in the stormy waters of the Southern Ocean. To deal with this problem, most cruises offer an on-board lecture programme, and with good lecturers this is an excellent way of learning about the fascinating history and wildlife of Antarctica.

Many cruises depart from Ushuaia on the southernmost tip of South America and include internal flights from Santiago or Buenos Aires and a day or two sightseeing in those capitals. Others depart from Punta Arenas in Chile, the Falklands, Hobart or Melbourne, Australia, or the South Island of New Zealand. Cruises departing from New Zealand and Australia visit the other side of the continent (not the peninsula).

Most cruise ships include luxury facilities such as saunas. Some even have swimming pools. They tend to operate an open-bridge policy, which means passengers are free to wander on and off the bridge and chat with the officers and Captain. All Antarctic cruisers are equipped with Zodiac inflatables to take passengers ashore (*see* **Practical A–Z**), and a few have helicopters. Twenty-four-hour daylight means you can take advantage of early-morning and late-night landings.

Shore excursions require a reasonable degree of agility as passengers are required to step in and out of Zodiac inflatable vessels on to uneven ground surfaces which may be wet.

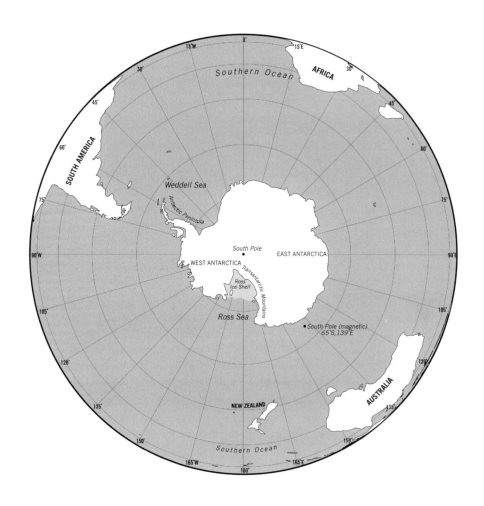

The Southern Hemisphere

Antarctica Seen in Relation to Surrounding Continents

When to Go

All cruises depart during the austral summer (there wouldn't be a lot of point in going during the polar night), beginning in November and continuing until March. The high season, which includes a hike in prices, generally runs from about 20th December to the beginning of February. Christmas bookings are at a premium, so if you want to spend the festive season in the south you'll have to book especially early.

Warning!

Conditions in Antarctica are extremely unpredictable. The extent of the pack ice, in particular, varies greatly from year to year, even from day to day, and this is a crucial factor in the success of cruises as it determines what landings you can make. It is impossible to predict how much pack ice will remain around the coast throughout the summer in any one year, and it does vary wildly. You must accept this risk. Don't blame the tour guide. If you are unlucky, you won't land as much as you might during an ice-free year. This doesn't mean the trip is spoiled, though; you can still see Antarctica in all its splendour from the deck of your ship.

Tour Operators

Which Tour Operator?

First of all, ensure that the tour company you are considering is a member of IAATO, the International Association of Antarctica Tour Operators. Once you have done that, all you can do is peruse the brochures in the usual way and try to assess which product best suits your needs and your budget. The Antarctic is still a maturing market for cruise companies and new products are always popping up and then disappearing without trace.

One factor to consider is group size. The ships vary a good deal, and if you prefer a more intimate scale you should pick your ship accordingly. Also, most cruises offer a guest lecture programme, and sometimes ensnare distinguished speakers and naturalists with extensive polar experience. If this is important to you, ask your tour operator who will be lecturing and guiding on your ship before you make your final decision.

There follows a selection of tour companies currently offering Antarctic cruises. This should be read as a guideline only. Itineraries change, companies withdraw products if they aren't profitable, tour operators disappear and new companies enter the market. The following companies all offer brochures, so ring up and ask for one if you are trying to decide which cruise is for you.

Prices

All prices are subject to change. They do not include airport taxes, travel insurance or tips to ships' crews. Some meals in South America may not be included: check your itinerary. If quoted prices include the flight from Europe or North America (and they usually do), this will be based on the economy-class fare. If you wish to pay a business-class supplement for an upgrade your tour operator should be able to arrange this. Dollar prices in this book all refer to US dollars.

Many cruises include a polar-weight parka in the price.

Abercrombie & Kent

Abercrombie & Kent Ltd, Sloane Square House, Holbein Place, London SW1W 8NS; © (0171) 730 9600; ☏ 730 9376; telex 8813352 Abkent G

Abercrombie & Kent International Inc, 1520 Kensington Road, Oak Brook, Illinois 60521, USA; © 708 954 2944 or 1-800 323 7308; ☏ 708 954 3324

This well-known and highly reputable adventure holiday company operates a ship specially built for the Antarctic, the *Explorer*. It can carry 104 passengers and has been cruising in Antarctica for 25 years. Currently three cruises are available, all boarding in Ushuaia in Tierra del Fuego, Argentina. One offers ten nights on board, the second, which also visits the Falklands, 11, and the third, which visits the Falklands and South Georgia, 15. On all these, five days are spent around the Antarctic peninsula with up to two landings a day. Certain dates in the first and the third of these trips offer an extra two days cruising the peninsula.

prices

Per-person prices, including flights from London to Chile or Argentina and bed-and-breakfast in Santiago or Buenos Aires before boarding, range from £4544 ($7043) for the most basic category cabin on an 11-night cruise (13 nights away in total) in low season, to £10,990 ($16,485) for a suite on the 15-night cruise (18 or 19 nights away) in high season. Two double-bed suites are available on the *Explorer*. Triple cabin prices are available on request. Early booking discounts available.

Aurora Expeditions

Aurora Expeditions, First Floor, 37 George Street, The Rocks, Sydney 2000, Australia; © (2) 9252 1033; ☏ (2) 9252 1373; email auroraex@world.net

Formerly called GMMS Polar Journeys, Aurora is an Australian expedition cruising company specialising in adventure travel in the polar regions. They operate cruises for small groups both in the peninsular area and around the part of the continent south of Australia (the latter type include visits to Australian scientific stations). What makes Aurora different from the competition is the fact that they run overnight camping trips—that is to say, passengers leave their ship and camp on the continent, usually for one night. This is often offered in conjunction with climbing and kayaking trips to the peninsula. Aurora's first scuba-diving trip is scheduled for the 1997/8 season.

The company has, during some seasons, offered trips in association with Quark Expeditions (*see* p.11).

An 11-day trip to the peninsula costs US$3800 per person for a twin cabin with a bathroom shared between two or three cabins. This price does not include airfare to Ushuaia. A 25-day trip from Fremantle (Western Australia) starts at US$10,600.

Journey Latin America

14–16 Devonshire Road, Chiswick, London W4 2HD, © (0181) 747 8315, ⊕ 742 1312, email tours@journeylatinamerica.co.uk

A tour company specializing in South America who also offer a large range of Antarctic cruises, on the Russian icebreaker *Kapitan Khlebnikov*, the smaller cruise vessels *Professor Khromov* and *Professor Molchanov*, and the large *World Discoverer*. All expedition staff are European and North American. The trips are mostly named after birds and include the 12-day Adélie, the 18-day Rockhopper, a circumnavigation of South Georgia called the Chinstrap, and the Macaroni, which adds the Chilean fjords to the experience.

Prices start from £2417 for the shortest trips, and go up to between £10,000 and £14,000 for the mammoth journeys on the Kapitan Khlebnikov, depending on cabin level. Most trips are in the middle range of £3000 to £5000 per person.

Marine Expeditions

The Cruise People, 88 York Street, London W1H 1DP; © (0171) 723 2450; ⊕ 723 2486; email cruise@dial.pipex.com. For advice and reservations in the UK also ring freefone (0800) 526 313

Marine Expeditions Inc., 13 Hazelton Avenue, Toronto, Ontario, Canada M5R 2E1; © (416) 964 9069 or (800) 263 9147; ⊕ (416) 964 2366

The Cruise People, 1252 Lawrence Avenue East, Suite 202, Don Mills, Ontario, Canada M3A 1C3; © (416) 444 2410; ⊕ 447 2628

Marine Expeditions is represented in the UK by The Cruise People, a company founded in Canada in 1972. It opened in London in 1992. This Toronto-based outfit claims to be the largest ship-based expedition company in the world. Currently operating six modern Russian and Estonian former research ships carrying up to 79 passengers each, Marine Expeditions specialize in remote areas.

They are currently offering three Antarctic cruises. These begin in Santiago (Chile) or Buenos Aires (Argentina), with flights to Ushuaia at the tip of South America for boarding. All three climax with three to four days cruising in the channels of the Antarctic Peninsula and the South Shetland Islands. You will visit an abandoned whaling station on Deception Island and, if possible, a scientific research station. All cruises try to get into Hope Bay, Paradise Bay, Half Moon and Paulet Islands.

The shortest Marine Expeditions cruise to Antarctica offers eight nights aboard and three on land in South America. An extended version is also available, increasing the nights on board to ten: this is worth considering as the extra two nights are spent in Antarctic waters. The second includes the Falkland Islands and is five days longer, and the third, which includes South Georgia as well as the Falklands, is a 24-day trip again including three nights in South America. Crews are primarily Russian or Estonian, with a sprinkling of North American and Europeans to liaise with passengers. Besides the almost standard lecture programme, Marine Expeditions give each passenger a handbook. The company are keen to show their commitment to the Antarctic environment. Recently they co-sponsored a clean-up of the Polish Arctowski research base on King George Island.

prices

If you buy from the Marine Expeditions catalogue, prices are in US dollars and include flights from North America to Santiago or Buenos Aires. Passengers from Europe will be allowed to deduct the cost of this flight from the package (approximately $490, or £316), and your UK tour operator representing Marine Expeditions will arrange a flight to South America to meet the other passengers. Remember—if you want to fly from the UK, you will have to add the cost of this flight to the package. Dollar prices, including flights from New York, Los Angeles, Miami, Toronto or Montreal, range from $2995 to $7995 (£1932 to £5158) and reflect a range of accommodation on board: forward- or sideways-facing suites, double cabins with two lower berths or an upper and a lower, and bathrooms either *en suite,* shared with the next cabin or shared with several cabins.

The Cruise People, the UK agent for Marine Expeditions, are currently offering return flights to Buenos Aires for £649 (arranged with Journey Latin America) and quoting a sterling price for the expeditions not including the flight ranging from £1901 to £5301.

All rates are per person, assuming shared occupancy of a cabin. Single occupancy is available at about 1½ times the published fare. Single travellers who indicate that they are prepared to share their cabin, however, are guaranteed the double-occupancy rate for that cabin category—whether or not a room-mate is available.

Note that there is a reduction of 10 per cent for payment in full six months prior to departure, and 10 per cent discount on consecutive cruises.

Mountain Travel/Sobek

Mountain Travel/Sobek, 6420 Fairmount Avenue, El Cerrito, California 94530, USA; © (510) 527 8100; ◉ 525 7710; email MTS-info@MTSobek.com; Web site http://www.MTBSobek.com

European sales office: 67 Verney Avenue, High Wycombe, Bucks HP12 3ND, England; © (01494) 448901; ◉ 465526; email PureAdventure@msn.com

An experienced company offering a range of expeditions in a 38-passenger Finnish-built research ship. Previous trips have included 'Kingdom of the Penguin', a 19-day tour taking clients to see as many as eight different species of penguin, including king colonies on South Georgia. 'Footsteps of the Explorers' is also 19 days. On this trip the ship traces the route of a number of early explorers, beginning around South Georgia on the trail of Captain Cook. Passengers land at Hope Bay on the tip of the peninsula. Both of these trips depart from Ushuaia, as does the 16-day 'Quest for the Circle', a cruise which heads further south down the peninsula than most trips. It aims to reach 66 degrees 33 minutes south—the Antarctic Circle.

prices

'Kingdom of the Penguin' costs from about US$6400 per person, not including airfares. 'Footsteps of the Explorers' costs from about US$6000 per person, also not including air fares.

Noble Caledonia

Noble Caledonia Ltd, 11 Charles Street, London W1X 8LE; ☎ (0171) 409 0376; ▣ 409 0834. 24-hour brochure answerphone ☎ (0171) 35 1424

This company offers a range of cruises to Antarctica in the *World Discoverer*, a ship built in Germany in 1974 and specially designed for cruising in icy waters. The company claims that no ship has more expedition cruising experience. The *World Discoverer* was the first cruise ship ever to transit the Northwest Passage from the Pacific to the Atlantic. The captain and crew are European and the passenger capacity is 138.

Trips on the *World Discoverer* include the 20-day 'Antarctica and the Chilean Fjords' (it comes in at 27 days from London, if you count in the suggested stopovers in Santiago or Buenos Aires). This includes four days around the Antarctic Peninsula and a visit to Elephant Island, where Shackleton left his men following the loss of their ship on the 1914 expedition. This cruise embarks at the Chilean port of Talcahuano and ends at Ushuaia in Argentina. An 11-day cruise just to Antarctica also includes Elephant Island. This is 17 or 18 days from London, on the same basis as the previous cruise. The ship visits the usual places on and above the Antarctic Peninsula. The company also offers a 16-day trip to Antarctica, the Falklands, South Georgia and the South Orkney Islands (22 days from London), and a 17-day expedition to Antarctica, the Falklands and the Chilean Fjords (22 days from London).

prices

Prices, not including air fare or hotel accommodation in Santiago or Buenos Aires, range from £2393 ($3709) for the 11-day cruise to Antarctica to £8118 ($12,582) for a top suite on the Antarctica, Falklands and Chilean Fjords trip. Noble Caledonia offer prices for air fare and hotel accommodation packages to South America from London to fit with the cruises. These range from £1048 ($1624) (if you require a single room, £1121 or $1737) to £1480 ($2294) (£1695 or $2627 for a single). All-in prices from London for the Antarctica, Falklands, South Georgia and South Orkneys trip begin at £5838 ($9048).

Noble Caledonia also book **Southern Heritage** Antarctic cruises, which depart from New Zealand and visit the other side of the continent (*see* p.14), **Quark** cruises (*see* p.11) and **Society Expedition** cruises (*see* p.13).

Noble Caledonia products are only available from the UK, but many of the ships they use are part-chartered by US companies. Noble Caledonia are happy to quote on tailor-made trips to suit US clients.

Ocean Adventures

Ocean Adventures, Two Jays, Kemple End, Birdy Brow, Stonyhurst, Lancashire BB7 9QY; © (01254) 826116; ℻ 826780; email ocean@birdquest.co.uk

See p.6 for Marine Expeditions in North America. The special Birdquest cruises are only available through the UK office

A UK-based company which books **Marine Expedition** cruises (*see* above) and also organizes special Antarctic birdwatching cruises on Marine Expedition ships. These are known as *Birdquest/Ocean Adventure* departures, and include Antarctica, the Falklands and South Georgia. The size of the group ranges from ten to an upper limit of 18, and the trip lasts 24 days, which includes four days in Chile and Argentina (including some bird-watching). A guest lecturer and bird expert accompanies the group. Highlights include nesting Wandering Albatrosses on South Georgia, the Adélie colony on Paulet Island and Manx Shearwaters around the warmer waters of the Falklands.

prices

Current brochure prices from London range from £3950 ($6122) to £5850 ($9067) per person.

Orient Lines

Orient Lines, 38 Park St, London W1Y 3PF; © (0171) 409 7500; ℻ 409 7525

Orient Lines, 1510 S.E. 17th St, Suite 400, Fort Lauderdale, Florida 33316, USA; © (954) 527 6660; ℻ 527 6657

It was the late Lars-Eric Linblad, the father of Antarctic cruise tourism, who pioneered the first passenger expedition to Antarctica. That was back in 1965. Much later, Linblad designed the *Marco Polo*'s first programme, and for several seasons the huge ship has been ploughing through the Southern Ocean to give a few hundred tourists their very own glimpse of paradise.

Marco Polo was built in Germany in 1965, refurbished in Denmark in 1993 and first went south in 1994. It can carry 850 passengers, but on Antarctic cruises it operates at about half this capacity. Seventy per cent of the 425 cabins have outside views. The crew are Filipino and the officers Scandinavian and British.

Orient Lines' itineraries range from 13 to 25 days. Their 'Expedition Antarctica' is a 16-day visit to the peninsula, boarding in Buenos Aires and disembarking in the Falklands. The shorter (13-day) peninsular cruises are virtually the same, without the Falklands component and without stopping at Buenos Aires on the way out (for these, passengers board the Marco Polo at Ushuaia).

The most spectacular trip on the Orient Lines Antarctic itinerary is undoubtedly the semi-circumnavigation. The journey takes 26 days (including flying time from and back to the UK), and includes the Ross Sea area with its historic huts and bases as well as the usual sites of the peninsula. The trip boards in Ushuaia, Argentina and ends up in Christchurch, New Zealand. It was first undertaken by Orient Lines in 1994 and bad luck with the pack ice meant that the passengers didn't get to see half the attractions in the brochure.

An even longer cruise on the *Marco Polo* is the 35-day Antarctica and New Zealand. This is the semi-circumnavigation listed above with a week of cruising around New Zealand at the end.

prices

An early-booking discount means you can obtain a five per cent saving. Prices all include round-trip flights from the UK and begin, with the five per cent saving, at £2993 ($4639) for the 13-day cruise. Prices for the semi-circumnavigation begin at £4935 ($7649), and with the week around New Zealand at the end they start from £5695 ($8827). A deluxe suite on the semi-circumnavigation costs from £10,950 ($16,972) per person.

Orient Lines are a cruise specialist and offer various add-ons which are worth looking into if you have a little time and more money to spare: on 'Expedition Antarctica', for example, you can begin your trip with two nights in Cape Town, then spend eight days cruising the South Atlantic to Buenos Aires to meet the rest of the group. This costs from about £570 ($883) more. If you opt for the semi-circumnavigation you can extend your holiday in New Zealand, or Australia, or both.

Ornitholidays

Wessex Travel and Ornitholidays Ltd., 1–3 Victoria Drive, Bognor Regis, West Sussex PO21 2PW, ✆ (10243) 821230, ✉ 829574

The longest-established birdwatching and natural history tour operator in the UK, Ornitholidays offer a 24-day Antarctic 'Wildlife and Photography Tour' in the *World Discoverer*. Photography advice as well as detailed bird information is available.

prices

Costs range from £5990 per person sharing in a lower-deck cabin, to £8990 for a suite. British Airways flights are included in the price.

Quark Expeditions

Quark Expeditions, 980 Post Road, Darien, CT 06820; ℃ (203) 656 0499/1-800 356 5699; ✆ (203) 655 6623; email 76255.3266@compuserve.com

Noble Caledonia (see p.8) book Quark cruises in the UK. They will quote prices in sterling. WildWings are also a UK agent for Quark Expeditions. Contact them at International House, Bank Road, Bristol BS15 2LX; ℃ (0117) 984 8040; ✆ 967 4444

This company offers cruises to both sides of the Antarctic. In the **peninsula** area (nearest South America), it runs voyages of 10, 12 and 19 days aboard three ships: the *Professor Khromov*, *Akademik Ioffe* and *Alla Tarasova*. All were built for polar and oceanographic research and have recently been refurbished. The crews are Russian. The smallest of the three, the *Khromov*, was built in Finland in 1983, and can take 36 passengers. The *Akademik Ioffe* was built in 1989 and has 42 cabins. The largest, the *Alla Tarasova*, was built in 1974 and has 51 cabins. All the voyages feature between four and six days in Antarctica, in the peninsula and South Shetland areas. The longest, 19-day trip includes South Georgia and the Falklands. Like most peninsula cruises, Quark tours include a visit to Paradise Bay on the Danco Coast, where a series of glaciers flows from the 10,000ft Foster Plateau. They also usually stop at Petermann Island, where the great French Antarctic explorer Jean-Baptiste Charcot overwintered in 1901 aboard the *Pourquoi Pas?*. It is home to the world's southernmost gentoo penguin colony.

Quark expeditions also uses the M.S.*Bremen* to take passengers to the **Ross Sea** area on the 23-day (from Tasmania) 'Adventure Antarctica' cruise. This includes a visit to the sub-Antarctic Macquarie Island (Australian territory); a landing at Cape Adare, the site of a huge Adélie penguin colony and the hut from Carsten Borchgrevink's 1898–1900 *Southern Cross* expedition; and a look around the Possession Islands off Cape Hallett. If possible, passengers will land at Terra Nova Bay and visit the Italian research base of the same name. The high point is Ross Island, where you will visit Scott's hut at Cape Evans, the hut from his previous expedition at Discovery Point, and Shackleton's Cape Royds hut. The Ross Island itinerary also includes a visit to the American base at McMurdo and the New Zealanders at Scott Base. The *Bremen*, commissioned in 1990, accommodates 164 passengers in 82 cabins. It was designed specifically for expedition cruising in polar waters.

Quark also offer circumnavigations and semi-circumnavigations of the continent in the *Kapitan Khlebnikov*. The first complete 12,000-mile clockwise **circumnavigation** for tourists (from and to the Falklands) took place on this ship in the austral summer season 1996–7, and it is an epic journey, surely the pinnacle of Antarctic tourism. Not only is this a rare event for tourists—it is one of fewer than a dozen circumnavigations of the continent ever to have taken place. During the two-month extravaganza, on-board helicopters allow unique sightseeing opportunities, and wildlife highlights include a number of emperor penguin colonies as well as the elephant seals of the Windmill Islands. When the ship arrives in McMurdo Sound helicopter excursions are scheduled over to the Dry Valleys on the continent opposite Ross Island. This is one of the most pristine natural laboratories in the world; it has not rained there for two million years. The circumnavigation itinerary also includes visits where possible to numerous bases, including the Japanese Syowa in Queen Maud Land, the Russian Molodezhnaya in Enderby Land and Australia's Mawson on the Mawson coast, the oldest continually operating base on continental Antarctica. Passengers also visit most of the historic huts (Scott's, Shackleton's and Mawson's included). In short, the trip not of one but of several lifetimes.

The *Kapitan Khlebnikov*, built in Finland in 1981, is a powerful working icebreaker (other cruise ships are ice-strengthened). It has been refurbished to a high standard and has 54 cabins and suites. All cabins have two lower berths and private bathrooms. The crew are Russian, and the chefs European.

The Quark **semi-circumnavigation** is a month-long 600-mile journey anti-clockwise from the Falklands to New Zealand. All the sites of the peninsula are offered, as well as the Ross Sea and Ross Island, the latter including Scott's two huts and Shackleton's hut. You should see at least ten species of penguin, including the emperor, and seven species of albatross. Each person is given up to 90 minutes of helicopter time. You will also visit several bases, including Scott, the New Zealand station. At the end the ship calls in at several sub-Antarctic islands belonging to Australia, affording further wildlife opportunities. Like the full circumnavigation, the group meets in Santiago and flies together to the Falklands to embark.

prices

Prices for the **peninsula** trips, in US dollars, not including air fares but including accommodation in Santiago, range from $3350 to $9590, the latter for a corner suite on the 19-day cruise to Antarctica, the Falklands and South Georgia. The sterling equivalent ranges between £2161 and £6187.

For the **Ross Sea**/M.S. *Bremen* trips, prices per person from Hobart (so not including air fares) range from $8890 (£5735) for a Deck 3 Twin to $16,490 (£10,638) for a Deck 7 Veranda Suite. Single occupancy rates are 1.7 times twin-share price. A limited number of triple-share cabins are available, and in these cases the third person pays fifty per cent of the twin-share rate.

The per-person brochure price for the **circumnavigation**, not including flights to the Falklands but including hotel accommodation for one night in Santiago prior to the flight to the Falklands, ranges from $29,900 for a triple share on one of the four lowest decks to $55,000 for a corner suite. Noble Caledonia quote prices not including flights ranging from £19,940 for a berth in a triple-share cabin to £36,670 for a corner suite. Single cabins can be requested at a supplement of 1.7 times the twin-share price. The group meets in Santiago.

The per-person brochure price for the **semi-circumnavigation**, not including flights to the Falklands but including hotel accommodation for one night in

Santiago prior to the flight to the Falklands, ranges from $12,900 for a triple share on one of the four lowest decks to $21,000 for a corner suite. Noble Caledonia quote prices not including flights ranging from £8,600 for a berth in a triple-share cabin to £14,600 for a corner suite. Single cabins can be requested at a supplement of 1.7 times the twin-share price. Noble Caledonia can arrange London-Santiago/Christchurch-London for £959 per person, and the Santiago-Falklands one-way fare is quoted as £300.

Radisson Seven Seas Cruises

Radisson Seven Seas Cruises, 11 Quadrant Arcade, 80–82 Regent Street, London W1R 6JB; ℂ (0171) 287 9060; ✆ 434 1410

Radisson Seven Seas Cruises, 600 Corporate Drive, Suite 410, Fort Lauderdale, Florida 33334; ℂ (0800) 333 3333

Currently planning nine luxury-standard cruises for 1997–8 that include the Antarctic Peninsula, the Falkland Islands and South Georgia to a greater or lesser extent, combined with sailing down the coast of Chile to Ushuaia in Argentina, travelling 'Cape to Cape' from Ushuaia to Cape Town, South Africa, spending Christmas Eve with the reindeer in Grytviken, South Georgia, or simply passing the entire cruise in Antarctic waters. The ships are the small M.S. *Bremen*, or the larger M.S. *Hanseatic*, both equipped to a high standard and carrying a super ice classification.

prices

The 22-night 'Fjords of Chile and Antarctica' trip starts at $7670 including flights from London, or $10,795 including flights from 79 American cities. Shorter cruises, such as the 11- or 12-day 'Antarctica and the Falkland Islands', start at $7295. 'Cape to Cape' costs start at $9795.

Society Expeditions

Society Expeditions, 2001 Western Avenue, Suite 300, Seattle, WA 98121, USA; ℂ (206) 728 9400/1-800 548 8669; ✆ (206) 728 2301

UK sales agents are Noble Caledonia (see p.8)

Owners of the *World Discoverer*, which is also used by Noble Caledonia. The ship is now an old Antarctic warhorse. The company's programme consists of variations on the peninsula–Falklands–South Georgia tour, sometimes with additional days cruising in the Chilean fjords. Eight departures are scheduled per season, and a typical cruise lasts 20 days. The *World Discoverer* spends the austral summer cruising in the south; the rest of the year it sails in Arctic and tropical waters. Berth allocations are often chartered by other companies.

Southern Heritage Expeditions

Southern Heritage Expeditions, P.O. Box 20-219, Christchurch, New Zealand;
✆ (03) 359 7711; ✆ 359 3311

Noble Caledonia Ltd, 11 Charles Street, London W1X 8LE; ✆ (0171) 409 0376;
✆ (0171) 409 0834. 24-hour brochure answerphone ✆ (0171) 355 1424

This company, registered in New Zealand in 1985, has a distinguished track record in the field of environment-friendly tourism, and has won the Air New Zealand Eco-tourism Award. Cruises to Antarctica include the 26-day 'World of Penguins' trip departing from the south of New Zealand and arriving back at Hobart, Tasmania. It includes a number of sub-Antarctic islands and as many as five days visiting the coast of George V Land on the Antarctic continent. This is one of the first parts of the coast to free itself of ice each year and so wildlife abounds. There is an opportunity to visit the hut of Sir Douglas Mawson, the Australian explorer who, on his 1911–12 expedition, was based at Commonwealth Bay in George V land. After leaving Antarctica, the ship stops at Macquarie Island, breeding ground of four species of penguin including the Royal.

Another Southern Heritage trip is the thirty-day 'South to Antarctica—The Ross Sea'. This trip departs from Hobart, Tasmania and arrives back at the south of New Zealand. It visits a range of sub-Antarctic islands, and Macquarie, and includes five days in the Ross Sea area, sailing as far south as any ship can and if possible visiting the American base McMurdo and the Kiwi base Scott, both on Ross Island. Visits are also made to the three historic huts on Ross Island (two built by members of Scott's expeditions and one by Shackleton—*see* **Antarctic Sights**). Sometimes it is possible to cruise to Terra Nova Bay and visit the Italian base of the same name. On payment of a supplement, qualified scuba-divers can dive with this package.

A third expedition, lasting 22 days, is called 'In the Footsteps of Scott and Shackleton', and it visits a number of areas where the men lived and worked. Historians are on board to provide lectures and guided tours of the huts. The trip starts and finishes at Invercargill in the south of New Zealand. It visits a number of sub-Antarctic islands *en route* and includes visit to American, New Zealand and Italian bases if possible.

All trips sail aboard *Akademik Shokalski*, a research vessel built in Finland in 1983 and subsequently converted. 38 passengers are accommodated, making these cruises much cosier than most. The crew are Russian.

prices

Per person prices from New Zealand range from $8687/£5792 for a twin cabin with shared facilities on the 'World of Penguins' to $10,980/£7720 for a suite on 'South to Antarctica'. Add $450/£290 per diver if you wish to dive. Single-person rate is 1.5 times the advertised rate except in the case of a suite, when the rate goes up to 1.8 times the advertised price.

Noble Caledonia (see p.8) can book Southern Heritage Expeditions from the UK. They are currently charging £1138 per person for the London–Christchurch return flight for 'In the Footsteps of Scott and Shackleton'; £1218 to fly to New Zealand from London and then back from Hobart to London for 'The World of Penguins'; and £1230 per person to fly from London to Hobart and back from New Zealand to London for 'South to Antarctica—the Ross Sea'.

Wildlife Worldwide

Wildlife Worldwide, 170 Selsdon Road, South Croydon, Surrey CR2 6PJ; ✆ (0181) 667 9158; ✉ 667 1960; email: wildlife@compuserve.com

A company catering for 'wildlife enthusiasts and lovers of wilderness'. All their trips visit the Antarctic Peninsula and start at 12 or 14 days; you can add the Falklands and South Georgia for 17- and 22-day trips respectively. They also offer to tailor-make a 'Falklands à la carte' trip for those more interested in penguins than icebergs. Trips depart from either Santiago or Buenos Aires.

prices

Prices start from £1625 per person in a twin cabin for the 12-day Antarctica trip, and from £2075 for the longer journeys.

WildWings

WildWings, International House, Bank Road, Bristol BS15 2LX; ✆ (0117) 984 8040; ✉ 967 4444

The WildWings bird and wildlife tours are sold exclusively through the UK office

One of the first UK companies to join IAATO, WildWings operates its own inclusive bird and wildlife tours. It is also a UK sales agent for the complete range of Quark Expeditions (see p.11). Tours vary from season to season, as do the ships chartered. A typical tour would be 'Antarctica and the Falklands', a 15-day UK to UK trip, which starts at £3465 per person inclusive ex-UK. Another popular choice is a 27-day 'Peninsula and Ross Sea' expedition which starts at £4935.

Zegrahm Expeditions

Zegrahm Expeditions, 1414 Dexter Avenue N #327, Seattle, WA 98109, USA; ✆ (206) 285 4000 or (800) 628 8747; ✉ (206) 285 5037; email zegrahm@accessone.com.

Eco-Expeditions is at the same address.

This company claims to be 'dedicated to offering an expeditionary adventure to the inquisitive traveller'. It is currently selling a 21-day 'Antarctica, South Georgia and the Falklands' trip, to and from Miami, and a 28-day 'Ultimate Antarctica', concentrating on the Weddell

Sea, also out of Miami. Other trips are available, including a jumbo-length 68-day circum-navigation. The company charter four different vessels.

How about seeing the millennium in on the ice? Zegrahm's special '2000 Antarctica' expedition will leave the US on 20 December 1999, fly to Chile, sail from Punta Arenas and return to Puerto Williams, a small port on Isla Navarino in Tierra del Fuego, on 5 January 2005. Christmas will be spent in the Falklands, and New Year's Eve in Paradise Bay. For more information, see the Zegrahm web site at www.zeco.com.

Zegrahm co-founders have also started Eco-Expeditions, a small company offering a 37-day trip called Antarctica: the Far Side. It departs from South Africa and visits a range of sub-Antarctic islands before making a semi-circumnavigation of the continent and ending up in Perth, Australia.

prices

The 21-day 'Antarctica, South Georgia and the Falklands' trip starts at $7990. 'Ultimate Antarctica' begins at $11,990. Prices are not available for the '2000 Antarctica' cruise; a deposit of $500 is required for a reservation, and this is fully refundable up to six months prior to departure. Antarctica: the Far Side costs from $18,850 per person.

Other Ways of Travelling South

Flying with Qantas

Contact Qantas or your local travel agent for details. In Melbourne, Australia, Croydon Travel work in association with Qantas on the Antarctic day trip: ☎ *(03) 9725 8555*

This 12-hour round trip in a 747 includes on-board videos and even talks. It has to, really—there might well be so much cloud that you can't see anything. You have to get yourself to Australia, and then expect to pay in the region of £500 ($775) for the trip. Qantas are currently running the service from 1 December to mid-February. Approximately six flights per season depart from Melbourne, four from Sydney and one from Perth.

If you are lucky with the weather you get good views of glaciers, penguin colonies and the Mount Melbourne volcano. About four of the twelve airborne hours are spent directly over the Antarctic.

Flying with Adventure Network International

Adventure Network International, Canon House, 27 London End, Beaconsfield, Bucks HP9 2HN; ☎ *(01494) 671808;* 📠 *671725. In Punta Arenas ANI are at 935 Arauco;* ☎ *(061) 247735;* 📠 *226167*

The UK office handles worldwide sales; there is no US sales agent.

You can also fly to Antarctica with the specialist Antarctic expedition airline Adventure Network International (ANI), the only company in the market. ANI, founded in 1985 by two Canadian mountaineers and a British pilot, operate out of Punta Arenas and their own Antarctic camp situated on the ice-cap at eighty degrees south, below the peninsula. This camp is called Patriot Hills. ANI have carried over 700 people to Antarctica. Their aircraft transport and provide logistical support for most private expeditions to and within Antarctica—notably skiers aiming for another record. They also offer a tourist service, however, and if your budget is extremely elastic this may be the best option.

All ANI services begin in Punta Arenas. You will be picked up from there and transported to Patriot Hills, the ANI camp near the southern edge of the Ellsworth Mountains, in a Hercules C-130. This takes about six hours. The camp has a team of staff including a doctor, and can accommodate 48 people. From Patriot Hills a Twin Otter plane will take you to your final Antarctic destination whenever the weather allows. Since 1988 ANI have offered a daytrip to the South Pole (a distance of 680 miles and also about six hours each way from Patriot Hills). You'll get about two hours there. Mountaineering packages up the Vinson Massif in the Ellsworth Range are also on offer—at 16,067ft (4897m), Vinson is the highest peak in Antarctica. ANI are creative: they pioneered the first ever trip to visit the emperor penguin colony on the Dawson-Lambton glacier. They can tailor-make Antarctic trips for you, and hope to have flights operating out of Cape Town from 1997.

In February 1997 ANI ran, for the first time, a commemorative crossing of South Georgia aboard the *Professor Khromov*. It took place to celebrate the eightieth anniversary of Ernest Shackleton's crossing of South Georgia during the aborted *Endurance* expedition of 1914–17 (*see* **History**, p.129). The trip, setting out from and returning to Ushuaia, took 20 days, of which eleven were spent on South Georgia itself. Members of the group had the option of retracing his steps in an arduous traverse across the island.

ANI is a Canadian company with an office in England. All their trips depend on a variety of factors, notably weather and aircraft availability. You can end up hanging around for a long time, so these holidays don't suit people with an office job. The company advise you not to book any important appointments for two weeks after your scheduled return date, just in case. The Vinson climb, for example, can take anything from two days to two weeks; ANI suggest an average of ten days from base to base.

You are required to provide all your own clothing, and a sleeping bag.

prices

All costs are to and from Punta Arenas. ANI prices are quoted in American dollars. A flight to the South Pole costs about $21,000 (£14,000) per person. The Vinson Massif climb is about $25,750 (£16,600). A visit to the emperor penguins is also about $21,000. You can go and stay at the Patriot Hills camp for as little as $10,750 (£6900), and while there you are offered a free 45-minute local flight in a Cessna. Prices for the commemorative crossing of South Georgia started, for those wanting to make the 3–6-day foot crossing, at US$9000 for a twin cabin without a bathroom. The price was a thousand dollars less for on-board adventurers.

Hitching a Ride with the Chilean or Argentinian Navy

The Chilean Navy supplies Chilean bases on the islands to the north of the peninsula. Occasionally, during the austral summer, a ship appears in Punta Arenas with cabin space for a handful of tourists. The cost is minimal—from about fifty US dollars (£32) a day including all meals. The problem is, no one can tell you when, if ever, such a ship might appear, and even if that fact becomes known, no one can tell you if it might be able to take tourists. It really is a case of pot luck, but if you hit the jackpot—well, you'll have the trip of a lifetime for next to nothing. But be warned—conditions on board are not luxurious. It might be worth taking some of your own food along with you. Go for plain stuff you can keep down even if your tummy feels funny. And pack some water-purifying tablets.

There's no point in even trying to find out anything about navy ships while you are in Santiago. You must go to Punta Arenas (there are flights from the capital at least three times a day). There you can start your research at the office of Sernatur, the Chilean tourism outfit. This will undoubtedly mark the beginning of several wild-goose chases calling at naval offices all over town.

The same applies to the Argentinian Navy, which departs from Ushuaia.

Punta Arenas and Ushuaia aren't bad places to get stuck—though both can be very rainy and windy, even in summer. There is plenty of accommodation. See the tourist offices: Waldo Seguel 689, Casilla 106-D, Punta Arenas, ✆ (061) 241330; open Monday–Friday. In Ushuaia: San Martín 660, ✆/✉ (0964) 24550; open seven days.

Other DIY Options from South America

There is always talk of both the Chilean and the Argentinian governments exploiting tourism in Antarctica by offering package tours including accommodation at their bases in the South Shetlands. This has happened in the past. See the tourist offices in the capitals or in Punta Arenas and Ushuaia.

Some budget cruises are available from Punta Arenas but again, you have to hang around or be in the right place at exactly the right moment—they sell out almost instantly. Ask at the tourist office (address above) which travel agents are currently specialising in Antarctica. Worth a shot if you have lots of time.

Occasionally, when a spare berth is available, a regular cruise vessel such as those listed earlier in this chapter will take a passenger at a big discount and at the last minute from South America.

Going Solo

Good luck! Many people have visited Antarctica in their own yachts. The peninsula is the favourite location. Start off by seeing how everyone else did it—then do it your way. Published accounts (see **Further Reading**, p.143–7) include *Between Two Poles* by Amyr Klink, and *Then We Sailed Away* by the Ridgeway family. You will need a lot of time, and either a lot of money or the Herculean patience required to drum up sponsorship. If you believe in the project enough, you will do it.

Visas

Antarctica is not a restricted political entity, and no country has a requirement for a visa. All territorial claims are in abeyance under the Antarctic Treaty. Some permits may be required in the future when the Environmental Protocol is in force.

You may need visas for countries you are visiting on your way south. Check with the embassies of the countries concerned.

For Chile, citizens of most countries require only a passport and tourist card. These cards are obtainable on aircraft heading for Chile. The card is surrendered upon departure. For Argentina, no visa is required by citizens of the US, Canada, UK and most other Western European countries, but all need passports. For New Zealand, all visitors must have a passport valid for six months beyond the expected time of departure from New Zealand, unless they are Australian citizens, in which case they need just a valid passport. Most people, including citizens of the US, Canada, the UK and other EC countries, do not require a visa.

Health and Travel Insurance

It is as important to insure yourself against misadventure on an Antarctic cruise as on any other trip. Your tour operators will recommend their own pet insurance company, or ask around for quotes.

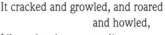

The Wedding Guest he beat his breast,
Yet he cannot choose but hear
And thus spake on that ancient man,
The bright-eyed Mariner.

'And now the STORM-BLAST came, and he
Was tyrannous and strong:
He struck with his o'ertaking wings,
And chased us south along.

With sloping masts and dipping prow,
As who pursued with yell and blow
Still treads the shadow of his foe,
And forward bends his head,
The ship drove fast, loud roared the blast,
And southward aye we fled.

And now there came both mist and snow,
And it grew wondrous cold:
And ice, mast-high, came floating by,
As green as emerald.

And through the drifts the snowy clifts
Did send a dismal sheen:
Nor shapes of men nor beasts we ken—
The ice was all between.

The ice was here, the ice was there,
The ice was all around:

It cracked and growled, and roared
                    and howled,
Like noises in a swound!

At length did cross an Albatross,
Thorough the fog it came;
As if it had been a Christian soul
We hailed it in God's name.

It ate the food it ne'er had eat,
And round and round it flew.
The ice did split with a thunder-fit;
The helmsman steered us through!

And a good south wind sprung up behind
The Albatross did follow,
And every day, for food or play,
Came to the mariners' hollo!

In mist or cloud, on mast or shroud,
It perched for vespers nine,
Whiles all the night, through fog-smoke
                    white,
Glimmered the white Moon-shine.'

'God save thee, ancient Mariner!
From the fiends, that plague thee thus!—
Why look'st thou so?'—'With my cross bow
I shot the ALBATROSS.'

from The Rime of the Ancient Mariner
by Samuel Taylor Coleridge

Practical A–Z

OPEN AIR TOILET

Birdwatching

It's worth boning up on the ornithology of the Southern Ocean as most people find bird-watching a richly rewarding activity when cruising in Antarctic waters. You will see a wide variety of seabirds, many of them unique to the region. Consider taking a small pair of binoculars, and a notebook. *See* **Wildlife**, pp.87–103.

Books

Most cruise ships have small libraries on board. *See* **Further Reading**, pp.143–6.

Children

If you are considering taking children on an Antarctic cruise, think carefully about the suitability of the venture. On-board activities such as lectures are geared to adults, and long days sailing in rough seas may not bring out the best in your offspring. Bear in mind too that there will probably be no other children, and bring along a supply of their own toys and books. Children over the age of ten, however, can get a lot from the Antarctic experience, especially if they are stimulated with information before and during the voyage. Most cruise companies offer a small reduction for children and can organise three-berth cabins.

Climate and Seasons

If you live in the northern hemisphere, Antarctic seasons are the opposite to your own. Summer runs from mid-October to mid-March, and winter from mid-April to mid-September. During summer it is permanently light in the interior of the continent, and even north of the Antarctic Circle dark nights are brief. Winter is the opposite: permanently dark in the heart of Antarctica with short spells of daylight further north. The brief cusps between summer and winter—the two months when the continent has a light cycle—can barely be described as 'spring' and 'autumn'. Such words seem indissolubly associated with green shoots and at least a few branches of burnished leaves. On the polar plateau in particular nothing visible happens between summer and winter except that it gets dark. Having said that, on the peninsula, in coastal regions and on the ice shelves, the advent of summer is a more perceptible event. The ice begins to crack, seals start popping up through their holes, Adélie penguins return and migratory birds fly in. Certain phenomena appear in the sky as a result of temperature inversion in the atmosphere.

The shift between seasons happens remarkably quickly in the south, and once the sun lifts itself above the horizon it stays up for approximately 20 minutes longer each day. You will almost certainly be visiting Antarctica during the southern summer (the opposite months to the northern summer) and so you won't experience the worst weather. However, it is going to be cold—perhaps as low as 20°C below freezing, but more likely two or three below. Around the peninsula area, and certainly on sub-Antarctic islands, it rains a lot.

The climate on the peninsula is milder than that of other continental areas, though even on Ross Island temperatures as high as plus five are not unknown in the summer months. In the peninsular area, expect average temperatures in December or January of between

Refrozen meltwater on the Nansen ice sheet in Victoria Land

ABOVE (LEFT TO RIGHT):
- *Building an igloo on the frozen water of the McMurdo Sound.*
- *The author in camp, baffled as usual by the VHF radio.*

BELOW (LEFT TO RIGHT):
- *Snowmobiles are used in science camps all over Antarctica. This one is towing a sledge full of gear.*
- *A Hägglunds tracked vehicle on the frozen McMurdo Sound, pursued by a VXE-6 helicopter.*
- *A twin otter plane leased by the American Antarctic Program stops at an abandoned underground science camp.*

BOTTOM: *The US Coastguard icebreaker* Polar Sea *pauses on its way through the frozen McMurdo Sound.*

RIGHT (TOP TO BOTTOM):
- *The Barne Glacier on the edge of Ross Island.*
- *Looking out from the author's tent, New Year's Day, Mackay Glacier.*

TOP: *Author in front of the Barne Glacier on the edge of Ross Island. Mount Erebus looms behind.*

BOTTOM: *One of the Dellbridge Islands in McMurdo Sound. They form part of the rim of an inundated volcanic crater.*

minus two degrees Celsius and plus two. The effect of the wind can be dramatic. It might be only zero degrees Celsius, but a wind of 35 miles an hour means a wind chill factor of –20° (*see* below). On South Georgia it is very likely to be warmer (summer temperatures occasionally reach a tropical 20 above), but it can be very wet and windy.

A distinctive feature of the Antarctic climate is its capacity to change quickly. White-outs, gales and blizzards can spring up in no time. It is important to develop patience and a Buddhist-like acceptance when dealing with the Antarctic climate. If you have had perfect weather for ten days and total white-out on your one day at Scott's hut, just try to maintain your karma. Antarctica is like that, and you can't change it.

How to Calculate the Effect of Wind Chill on Temperature

wind speed	5mph/8kph	10mph/16kph	15mph/24kph	20mph/32kph	25mph/40kph	30mph/48kph	35mph/56kph	40mph/64kph
				Equivalent temperature in °F/°C				
50/10	48/9	40/4	36/2	32/0	30/-1	28/-2	27/-3	26/-3
40/4	37/3	28/-2	22/-5	18/-8	16/-9	13/-10	11/-11	10/-12
30/-1	27/-3	16/-9	9/-13	4/-15	0/-17	-2/-19	-4/-20	6/-21
20/-6	16/-9	4/-15	-5/-21	-10/-23	-15/-26	-18/-28	-20/-28	-21/-29
10/-12	6/-14	-9/-23	-18/-28	-25/-32	-29/-34	-33/-36	-35/-37	-37/-38
0/-17	-5/-20	-21/-29	-36/-38	-39/-39	-44/-42	-48/-44	-49/-45	-53/-47
-10/-23	-15/-26	-33/-36	-45/-43	-53/-47	-59/-51	-63/-53	-67/-55	-69/-56
-20/-28	-26/-32	-46/-43	-58/-50	-67/-55	-74/-59	-79/-62	-82/-63	-85/-65
-30/-34	-36/-38	-58/-50	-72/-58	-82/-63	-88/-67	-94/-70	-98/-72	-100/-73
-40/-40	-47/-44	-70/-57	-85/-65	-96/-71	-104/-76	-109/-78	-113/-81	-116/-82
-50/-45	-57/-49	-83/-64	-99/-73	-110/-79	-118/-83	-125/-87	-129/-83	-132/-91
-60/-51	-68/-55	-95/-70	-112/-80	-124/-86	-133/-92	-140/-96	-145/-98	-148/-100

Actual thermometer reading in °F/°C

Temperature Conversion Rule

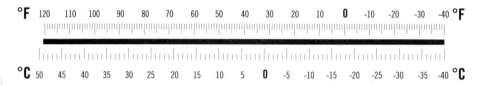

°F	120	110	100	90	80	70	60	50	40	30	20	10	0	-10	-20	-30	-40	°F

°C	50	45	40	35	30	25	20	15	10	5	0	-5	-10	-15	-20	-25	-30	-35	-40	°C

Clothing

Try to model the clothing you pack for Antarctica on the principle of loose-ish layers. Think in three basic categories: inner, intermediate and outer.

The **inner layer** should consist of thermal longjohns and a long-sleeved vest. These are usually made of a fabric such as polypropylene. Besides clinging to the body and trapping air, this layer also draws the moisture of sweat away from your skin without conducting the heat of your body away at the same time. Avoid cotton, as it absorbs water. This kind of thermal underwear can be purchased at expedition shops or good, large department stores. Some specialist companies offer a mail-order service if you find it hard to get to a shop.

The **intermediate layer** is basically your insulation. You will probably need two garments on the top half of your torso—for example a heavy shirt and a pile fibre jacket. This latter item would actually be a very useful item for the whole of your trip—they are excellent, for example, for short visits out on deck when cruising through the Southern Ocean. Often known as fleeces, pile jackets are really cosy and they can be easily taken on or off. They have pockets, and you can get plenty of other clothes underneath them. Your trousers should be heavy-duty—take advice from your outdoor equipment shop (most of these also offer a mail-order service and excellent catalogues). In general, synthetic fabrics are best for the intermediate layer, though wool is a good substitute.

The **outer layer** is going to protect you against wind and rain. Have a look around—you will soon find the best parka or anorak for you. The ones made to cope with extreme conditions (there are a number on the market) will all be warm, hooded, waterproof and, as far as it is possible, windproof. Note that many cruise companies offer a polar parka as part of the package. You should also take a pair of waterproof overtrousers. If you are on a cruise you will appreciate these for deck wear during the passage.

Moving on to the extremities, take half a dozen pairs of thick socks, and a really good pair of waterproof boots which extend above your calves. (If you go on the ice for a number of hours it is a good idea to carry a spare pair of socks in your pocket or daypack.) It is important to keep your head warm as the body loses a lot of heat through the head. In addition to a regular cold-weather hat, you might like to invest in a fleece balaclava which you can wear under any other kind of headgear. They are excellent, as when used in conjunction with sunspecs or (even better) goggles they leave virtually no flesh exposed to the wind. Another useful product (and this one has the advantage of costing very little) is the fleece headband. These are surprisingly efficient at keeping a bit of you warm, and if you have a lot of hair they also keep that out of the way.

Gloves are a vital part of your kit as hands are prone to frostbite. Don't skimp on this item. You'll need at least two pairs, probably a pair of polypropylene liners and then a proper expedition-strength pair on top. Gloves are notoriously easy to lose, so consider attaching them to your parka with cord.

This might sound complicated, but don't worry. You should look upon it as part of the adventure of your trip. If you have bought a ticket on a cruise the company will offer you advice before you go, and the staff in outdoor-clothing shops are always a mine of information. Remember: nothing tight-fitting, and don't buy a white parka as it makes it hard for others in your group to spot you in poor conditions.

As for indoor gear, if you are cruising your ship will be centrally heated, so you should take casual, comfortable clothes for wearing inside. Antarctic cruises operate in the expedition spirit and on most you are not required to dress for dinner as if you were on the *QE2*. Some do have formal nights, however, or at least require men to wear a jacket and tie for special dinners; check your itinerary. If you are scheduled to visit a base, make sure you can strip off layers easily, as most bases are quite hot inside.

You might find this hard to believe, but you should pack a swimming costume. If you stop at Deception Island you may have the opportunity to take a dip in the hot springs. Some of the more luxurious cruise ships have a sauna, and you may prefer to wear a swimsuit in it. There is also a wonderful swimming pool in Stanley in the Falklands, and if you stop there at the end of your Antarctic adventure you may be desperate for exercise.

Environmental Awareness

The Environmental Protocol to the Antarctic Treaty includes regulations to reduce the amount of waste produced or disposed of in Antarctica in order to minimise the effect on the environment. What this means in practice is that you should take all waste, no matter how small or 'biodegradable', back on to your ship. On board you will be instructed as to where waste must go. Each vessel has its own rules. Used batteries are particularly prone to contaminate, so be vigilant with them.

You might bear the problem of waste disposal in mind when you pack. Remove all surplus packaging (for example the cardboard boxes around film canisters, or cellophane around new clothes) before you leave home. Industry statistics have revealed that every man, woman and child on a cruise produces seven pounds of rubbish each day.

On land, you must be very careful where you tread. Antarctic mosses take hundreds of years to grow just one inch, and your clodhoppers can destroy them in a second as you charge across the ice to get a shot of a penguin feeding its young. *See* 'How to Approach Wildlife', p.103.

All members of IAATO, the International Association of Antarctica Tour Operators, commit their staff and passengers to adherence to the Guidelines of Conduct for Antarctic

Visitors established by the Antarctic Treaty Consultative Parties (*see* pp.141–2). Preventative conservation measures have been stepped up since the disastrous episode of the *Bahia Paraiso*, an Argentinian cruise ship which sank off the peninsula in 1989, spilling its oil into the surrounding sea. Cruise ships often carry official 'observers' on board, usually representing a signatory government to the Antarctic Treaty.

Above all, use your common sense. Although the Antarctic Treaty has made certain provisions for tourism, rules governing tourist activities in the region have evolved in an *ad hoc* manner and remain incomplete.

Food and Drink

As it isn't possible to purchase food and drink in Antarctica, and nothing grows, all your needs will be gratified by your cruise ship or, if travelling privately, you'll have to take it yourself. Most ships run short of fresh food after a fortnight away from port, so be prepared to eat more preserved food than usual. If you are intending to spend a number of hours on the ice it is a good idea to have a high-energy snack in your pocket—dried fruit is a good one, or the muesli-type 'health' bars on the market. Refined sugar will do (chocolate is the most popular form). Above all it is vitally important to drink large quantities of water in Antarctica as the air is so dry you can easily become dehydrated. Pack a plastic water-bottle. Alcohol has the reverse effect, as it *dehydrates*.

Health

Cold injuries fall into two broad categories: general (hypothermia) and local (frostnip and frostbite). Hypothermia is a drop in body-core temperature from its normal 37°C to or below 35°C. Symptoms include confusion, lethargy, chronic shivering and unsteadiness. It can kill—but if you dress properly and follow safety instructions you have nothing to fear. Frostbite is a local freezing of tissue, usually on extremities such as hands, feet, nose or ears. Frostnip is its milder version. The first symptoms are coldness, followed by numbness.

One way of preventing the onset of cold-weather injuries is to operate a similar buddy system to that of scuba divers: travel in pairs and keeping checking each other for symptoms. Look at your partner's face to check for white patches (a symptom of frostnip), and if you see him or her stumbling around (a symptom of hypothermia) suggest they stop and warm up for a while—perhaps go back to the ship for a hot drink. If you feel cold, get to shelter.

Cold burn from exposed metal surfaces is a danger. Be vigilant. Keep your glove-liners on even if you can bear to have your gloves off.

Sun

The increase in ultraviolet light in Antarctica means that the sun is dangerous even on cloudy days. A high-protection-factor sunblock on exposed flesh is essential at all times. Carry it in your pocket. Lipsalve with sun protection is also necessary. Small tubes, and lipsalve, are difficult to handle with cold hands and impossible with gloves. To avoid dropping them in the snow and becoming chilled while you fiddle about, try attaching them to the zip tag of your parka or anorak with string (you can attach the string to the tube with insulating tape).

You must also be careful to avoid snow-blindness, which is basically sunburn of the eye caused by over-exposure to ultraviolet light. The symptoms are stinging eyes, as if filled with grit, followed by weeping and reddening. As in the case of sunburn, do not be beguiled into thinking that snow-blindness cannot strike on an overcast day—it can. Wear your glasses or goggles if you feel you need them. Again, do attach some kind of strap to your glasses so you can carry them around your neck.

Vaccinations

Antarctica does not appear on the brightly coloured charts on the doctor's wall telling you what shots you need before you go on holiday. There are no rampant diseases. You needn't fear malaria (I wouldn't fancy a mosquito's chances in those temperatures). A tetanus toxoid inoculation is considered a good idea for any form of travel, however, and a booster provides immunity for ten years. Other jabs depend very much on where you are travelling *en route* to Antarctica—consult your doctor or local immunisation centre once you know your itinerary.

Most cruise ships have an on-board doctor, but it's worth packing your own private first aid kit. Take aspirin or other pain relief tablets, stomach settlers, sticking plaster for minor abrasions and so on, plus of course a good supply of any regular medication you take. Pack sea-sickness pills if you have the slightest suspicion that you might need them. Acupressure wristbands are an effective weapon against sea-sickness, and have no side effects. You can buy them at any good chemist.

Laundry

Most cruise ships have a laundry facility and you can simply leave clothes in a bag in or outside your cabin and they will be returned to you clean. Modern high-tech fabrics such as polarfleece tend to dry quickly, which is a boon in the cramped space of a cabin if you wash out items yourself.

Mail

You can only send mail from Antarctica if you are calling in at certain bases. Rothera has a British Antarctic Territory post office which has its own stamps. You can purchase these stamps and post letters, cards and packages from Rothera—they will be sent on via the Falklands. Don't swamp the Rothera staff; they have a limited mail capacity. At Scott Base on Ross Island you can purchase New Zealand stamps and send mail, which is then routed through Christchurch. Australian, Chilean and Argentinian bases have similar arrange-ments. American bases do not send tourist mail. As nobody is ever quite certain when to expect planes, and weather can torpedo the best-laid plans, allow three or four weeks for anything you post to reach its destination.

Maps

It is difficult to get hold of really good Antarctic maps—the ones produced by the US Geological Survey are very useful, especially the 1:250,000 Reconnaissance Series (write to US Geological Survey at either Denver, Colorado 80225, USA, or Reston, Virginia 22092, USA). The British Antarctic Survey, in co-operation with SPRI, SCAR and the RGS, publish an excellent Topographical Database map (1:10,000,000) which you can purchase for £5 (write to the British Antarctic Survey, High Cross, Madingley Road, Cambridge CB3 0ET). For the peninsular area BAS also publish an excellent 1:3,000,000 map called British Antarctic Territory which includes South Georgia and the South Sandwich Islands. Australian-made maps of Antarctica are available from the Australian Surveying and Land Information Group (AUSLIG), AUSMAP Sales, PO Box 2, Belconnen, Australian Capital Territory, 2606 Australia. As well as the maps included in this guide, many of the books listed in the **Further Reading** section at the back of this book, pp.143–6, have maps on which you will be able to trace your route, and all cruise ships are well equipped.

Money and Banks

It is not strictly true to say that there are no banks in Antarctica, as the Chileans have erected one at their base on King George Island. This branch of the Banco de Crédito e Inversiones is unlikely to be much good to the tourist, however. It consists of a kind of mobile home and was brought south largely to prove just how very much an ordinary part of Chilean territory King George Island is. There is no currency in Antarctica—no monetary system at all. You can purchase things at a few bases (*see* p.30) and the currency you use depends on the base. For any trip of this kind it is worth having a small amount of US dollars cash about your person. There are very few places where it won't be accepted.

Most cruise ships operate a chit system on board so passengers are not obliged to carry money. Accounts are settled at the end of the voyage. If a ship does accept cash, it is likely to be US dollars. Check with your tour operator before departure.

Photography

This is a vastly popular pursuit with all visitors to the Antarctic. After all, you'll probably never be there again, and the chances are that your family and friends back at home will never go at all. During the Antarctic summer you can achieve spectacular results with any kind of camera. It is true that cold temperatures slow up batteries—ten minutes can ruin them if it's −10°C, but this won't pose a problem to your camera in summer as long as you don't leave it outside for too long.

The Camera

Choose a camera with which you are comfortable, not one that needs endless fiddling. The body of most modern cameras will operate satisfactorily to −20°C, though the digital lead-crystal displays fade as the temperature falls. New or recently serviced autofocus lenses function down to about −15°C, although you may find they are mechanically slower. During the winter, temperatures are unsuitably low for autofocus cameras as they overtax batteries. You may consider taking a pair of thin glove-liners made of cotton or silk which you can keep on when you are lining up shots. If you buy a new camera for the trip it is worth shooting off a few rolls at home before you go, to familiarize yourself.

Taking Care of your Camera

Keep all your photographic equipment well protected throughout your journey. If you are carrying batteries around as you walk on the ice, stow them well inside folds of clothing. To protect yourself against cold burn, before leaving home you might like to cover the exposed metal parts of your camera with insulating tape. Also, if you use lens caps, it's worth attaching them with string to the body of the camera, otherwise you'll end up scrabbling around in the snow. If you drop any of your gear, don't attempt to blow off the snow—your breath will freeze. Shake or brush it off.

Condensation

This can be a danger to the Antarctic photographer, as it forms when moist warm air hits a cold surface. In Antarctic temperatures this happens every time you bring your camera inside the ship's cabins. To guard against it, try leaving your equipment in an unheated room on board before bringing in to a heated environment—letting it down gently, if you like. If this is not possible (and it often won't be) keep the camera in an airtight plastic bag, in which case the condensation will form on the outside of the bag.

Film

If you are shooting in black and white, a slow-to-medium speed copes best with the unusual intensity of light in an Antarctic summer. Try between about 25 and 125 ASA. For colour transparencies most of the regulars seem to use Kodachrome 25 and 64 ASA. If you are used to the standard 100 and 200 ASA colour print film, don't be afraid to use it—it has produced excellent results for many people.

Don't worry about taking too much film—you'll always find a buyer on board in the unlikely event of ending up with a surplus, and if you stop at a base the inmates will be clamouring for it as everyone in Antarctica takes more pix than they ever thought possible. Almost certainly, though, you just won't be able to stop snapping yourself.

Filters

Keep a skylight or ultraviolet filter on each lens—it helps counteract the increased ultra-violet radiation in Antarctic regions. It's well worth experimenting with other filters too: a red one with black and white film can work brilliantly for a vast southern sky, and a polarizing filter can help with the brilliant colours if you are shooting in colour.

Bracketing

Don't trust your light meter in these bright conditions. 'Bracket' each shot with alternatives at wider and narrower f-stops. This will increase your chances of success.

Video Cameras

These have proved successful in Antarctica and many cruise passengers take them along. Pack plenty of batteries—their life is dramatically reduced by the cold, and to conserve them it's also worth being stingy with techniques such as zooming which take up a lot of battery power. Lithium batteries are best suited for cold conditions, if available and if your camera takes them. Be aware of the dangers of exposed metal on flesh.

Photographing Wildlife

Penguins and seals have no land predators in Antarctica so they show no fear of human beings. You will be able to get much closer than you expect. Be aware, however, that this can cause them stress which you can't detect. IAATO guidelines recommend that you maintain a distance of at least fifteen feet from penguins, all nesting birds and most seals, and fifty feet from fur seals (*see* 'How to Approach Wildlife', p.106.)

And finally—it's worth carrying a small notebook to jot down what you are taking and where. You'll never remember the details when you get home.

Safety

Antarctica is one of the most lethal environments known to man. If you are on a cruise, it is essential to follow the rules laid down by your guide at all times. Wandering out of sight of the group to get that special shot can turn very nasty indeed if the weather changes fast—and it is in the habit of doing so. People have got lost in white-outs within ten feet of a building (this is why white clothing is so unsuitable). Familiarize yourself with the code of practice your tour company follows.

Scuba-diving

Two cruise companies offer this facility in Antarctic waters. *See* Aurora Expeditions and Southern Heritage Expeditions, **Travel**, pp.5 and 14.

Shopping

No malls here. On this trip you have the ultimate excuse for not taking gifts back home. Some bases offer a small selection of souvenir goods for sale; the best is undoubtedly at the Scott Base shop on Ross Island, so if your ship stops there you'll be able to stock up on souvenirs. The Scott Base shop sells T-shirts, postcards, mugs—the usual range of tourist goods, all bearing Antarctic logos, photographs and slogans. New Zealand dollars and US dollars are accepted, as are travellers' cheques and the usual credit cards. McMurdo has a much bigger shop, which takes US dollars, but its range is far smaller. At Rothera a small stock of items available to tourists includes philatelic material, T-shirts and hideous ties.

Unofficial shops operate on a few bases, and you will be made aware of these if you go ashore. Staff at the Russian station on King George Island, for example, have been known to produce chunks of amber from the homeland for the benefit of tourists. US dollars go down very well.

Shipboard shops are a feature of most cruise vessels, and they operate on the chit system. Besides batteries, film, chocolate and other practical items they usually stock books on Antarctica, items of polar clothing and gifts such as calendars.

The best range of Antarctic merchandise in the world is sold at the Antarctic Centre in Christchurch, New Zealand (situated at the airport). Here you will find everything from boxer shorts with an all-over rookery print to cut-glass whales and a vast array of fluffy penguins. The shop is not cheap but the goods are all high quality. If you are not passing through Christchurch you can send off for a catalogue and order by mail: the address is International Antarctic Centre, PO BOX 14-001, Christchurch, New Zealand, (0064 3) 353 7799. They will mail anywhere in the world.

Duty-free shopping is available in Ushuaia. Look out for leather goods.

Smoking

If you smoke on the ice, take your cigarette ends back on board in your pocket, as they harm the environment (skuas might eat them, to start with). If you visit a base, very strict rules apply because of the tremendous danger of fire in the tinder-dry Antarctic climate. Usually there is one small smoking room on a base, sometimes not even that. Several bases have burnt down. Remember that even if everyone escapes from the fire, they may then die of exposure. So don't smoke on or near bases. And as for the historic huts—don't be the one who sends Scott's hut up in flames. It really would spoil your holiday.

Some cruise ships have smoking cabins and designated smoking areas.

Telephones

Assume there aren't any. Some bases have telephones of one kind or another, but they are very precious to the occupants of the base—some of them will be away from home for two and a half years. If you are on a ship which is calling in to a base, don't expect to be able to avail yourself of this facility.

Most cruise ships have satellite telephones on board which passengers may use. This is an expensive service (about fifteen US dollars per minute) which cannot be relied on. Fax transmissions are also available on the same basis, and you may be able to receive both telephone calls and faxes. There is a charge for incoming calls, and it is not possible to receive reverse charge (collect) calls.

Some ships have an email facility available to passengers. Enquire before departure if this is important for you; but again, don't rely on it.

Time

You will almost certainly be visiting Antarctica during a period of 24-hour daylight. It isn't a country, with political borders, so it doesn't run a certain number of hours before or after Greenwich Mean Time. It keeps its own time.

The bases, however, have to establish a system to facilitate communal living, and this is passed on to field parties so they can call in each day as a safety check at an appointed hour. Most bases keep the time of the country which is geographically nearest. Thus Rothera Base (UK) keeps Falklands time (four hours behind GMT); McMurdo (US), Scott (New Zealand) and Terra Nova Bay (Italy) keep New Zealand time (twelve hours ahead of GMT); Bellingshausen (Russia) keeps Chilean time (three hours behind GMT). The Australian stations are regulated by Eastern Australian Standard Time (EAST): Mawson is four hours behind EAST, Davis three, Casey two and Macquarie Island is on EAST. During the daylight-saving period in Australia, these stations are a further hour behind EAST.

Tourist Information

Your tour ship will have plenty of information available in the form of literature and on-board experts. Most issue daily information sheets listing scheduled activities (such as lectures), shore excursions, notes about interesting sights to be observed that day, and weather information. Make use of the **Further Reading** section at the back of this book to mug up on subjects that interest you before you go. If you are calling in at any bases you will be given a tour and the guide will be happy to answer any questions; you will almost certainly have the opportunity to chat with other base personnel during the visit. Make the most of it—they enjoy seeing new faces. You might bear their isolation in mind before setting out from home and include a few gifts in your luggage. Up-to-date magazines go down well, or the latest paperback, and they would certainly appreciate a bar of luxury chocolate or a bottle.

Whalewatching

This is a natural feature of any passage though the Southern Ocean. Whales exert an endless fascination for most of us, perhaps because of their vast size. You will almost certainly see whales fluking round your ship. On a cruise ship the crew will be keeping a lookout too, and if possible they alert passengers through the tannoy system when whales are spotted. If you see any whales, do tell the bridge about it so that an announcement can be made. You should always have at least your fleece or anorak and a pair of gloves near at hand so you can nip out on deck. You will learn tell-tale signs, for example a flock of seabirds picking at the water is often an indication that whales are churning up krill to feed. *See* **Wildlife**, p.99–101, for information about the kinds of whales you are likely to see.

Zodiacs

These motorized, inflatable boats are an essential piece of equipment on all cruise ships to Antarctica, as they take passengers ashore. Zodiacs were developed by Jacques Cousteau, and they are sturdy and safe. They seat twelve to fourteen passengers and cruise at an approximate speed of four knots. Wear waterproof gear, as it can be a splashy ride, and you may have to step into water up to ten inches deep when you land. While Zodiacs do demand a minimal degree of agility they are not difficult to get in and out of, and you will be assisted by your guide. All passengers are requested to put on a lifejacket before boarding a Zodiac.

South American Departure Points

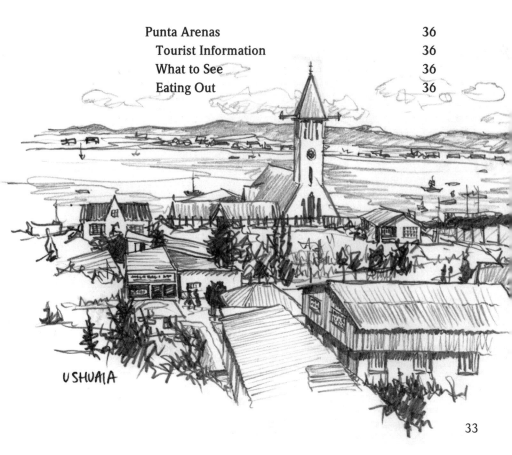

USHUAIA

Cruises to Antarctica or to the Falkland Islands may depart from a variety of southern hemisphere towns, such as Cape Town in South Africa or Hobart in New Zealand. The most common departure points, however, are those nearest to the continent, on the southernmost tip of South America: Ushuaia in Argentina or Punta Arenas in Chile. Even cruises leaving from other locations will usually stop for a day or so on the South American coast, and passengers will be allowed to disembark and explore.

Ushuaia

The island province of Tierra del Fuego at the very bottom of South America is separated from the mainland by the narrow Strait of Magellan. Tierra del Fuego is actually an archipelago composed of one big island (divided between Chile and Argentina) and many smaller ones, and the fast-growing city of Ushuaia, with a population approaching 50,000, is its capital. Before Magellan's exploration in 1520, the area was inhabited by the Yamana, Alacaluf, Selk'nam and Haush peoples, living by land-hunting or by fishing. In 1832 Charles Darwin sailed into the green waters of the Beagle Channel, and the slow but continuous settlement by Europeans corresponded, unsurprisingly, with the decline of the native Fuegians: by 1910 there were only 150 left. In 1870 a British-based Anglican mission was established in Ushuaia, and Argentina decided in 1898 to follow the European idea of colonising with criminals: the first 34 prisoners built a prison east of Ushuaia which took them from 1902 to 1920 to construct, though it remained open only until 1947. From the 1950s the town has been an important base for the Argentine navy, underpinning by its presence the country's claims to Antarctic territory, and, as well as tourism, the economy is supported by timber-cutting, fishing and electronics.

Tourist Information

A helpful, English-speaking tourist office can be found at 660 San Martín, ☎ (0901) 32000/24550, ✉ 24550, open Mon–Fri 8.30am–8.30pm, Sat and Sun 9am–8pm. The office has a web page on www.satlink.com/ushuaia/dmturush.

Around the Town

The 'city at the end of the world' has a distinctive topography of mountains, sea, glaciers and forest which present opportunities for an unusually wide range of activities, including skiing and walking in the National Park of Tierra del Fuego. If you only have a few hours on land, however, you will probably want to concentrate your activities on exploring the steep streets of the city centre, a mixture of modern architecture and old wooden and tin houses with sloping red roofs. Along the north edge of the Beagle Channel runs Avenue Maipú, and Avenue San Martín, full of hotels and restaurants, is parallel just to the north; a stroll along the length of these two streets will give you a good idea of its atmosphere, taking you past the most important museums and civic buildings and a wide range of late

19th/early 20th-century family houses; or you could pop into the tourist office (*see* above) and follow some or all of the 'city tour' suggested in their official glossy brochure *Ushuaia.*

The Museum at the End of the World

The **Museo Territorial**, Maipú y Rivadavia, ✆ 21863 (*open Mon–Sat 4pm–8pm; adm*) was originally built as the private residence of governor Manuel Fernandez Valdés in 1903. In 1911 it was bought by the National Bank, and it became a museum in 1978. It contains early photographs, artefacts and testimonies of native Fuegians, displays of ship-wrecks, the stories of early settlers and prisoners, natural history, and replicas of an early general store and bank. It's well worth the small admission charge.

Short Excursions Out of Town

If you find yourself with a day or even a half-day to spare, several out-of-town excursions are possible. Sail down the Beagle Channel to see the sealions on **Isla de Los Lobos** or the birds on **Isla de Pájaros**; trips leave from the tourist jetty on Avenue Maipú, last from 2½ to 4 hours, and cost around US$40 for the return journey. You can also take a boat from the tourist jetty past these islands and on to **Estancia Harberton**, where there is a penguin rookery. The *estancia* is the oldest on the island, and the return journey is made by bus through forest and open countryside. Trips take 6–9hrs. If you want a break from boats, hike, or take a bus, from the west end of Avenue San Martín into the **National Park** as far as the magnificent **Glacier Martial**; the 7km walk takes about 2–3hrs and the views of the bay are stunning. There is a chair-lift and winter sports at the glacier.

The tour operator **Rumbo Sur**, San Martín 342, ✆ 21139, offers a variety of day hiking or cycling excursions. For trout-fishing trips contact the **Asociación de Caza y Pesca**, Maipú y 9 de Julio; in winter you could ice-skate at the rink in the gymnasium (ask at the tourist office).

Shopping

A good souvenir of Ushuaia would be a carving made from the wood of the *lenga* trees which line the Paso Garibaldi on the way to Río Grande. If you can, buy photographic film in Chile, as Ushuaia is very expensive.

Eating Out

Mustacchio, San Martín y Godoy, ✆ 21601 (*expensive*) is renowned in Ushuaia for both its food and service, as is **La Casa de Los Mariscos**, San Martin 232, ✆ 21928 (*expensive–moderate*). **Tia Elvira**, Maipú 349, ✆ 24725 (*expensive*) is a popular seafood restaurant for which booking is essential. **Volver**, Maipú 37, ✆ 23977 (*moderate*) has good food and unusual decor. If you make the trip out to the Glacier you could eat at **Restaurant Hotel Las Hayas**, Camino Glaciar Martial Km.3, ✆ 30710 (*moderate*). Slightly cheaper food options include **Club Nautico Ushuaia**, Maipú y Belgrano, ✆ 24028, **Kaupe**, Roca 470, ✆ 22704 and **Las Lengas**, Goleta Florencia 1722, ✆ 23366; and there is an assortment of small cafés along the waterfront if you just want a quick bite.

Punta Arenas

On the mainland, just across the Magellan Strait from Tierra del Fuego's Isla Grande, is Chile's most southerly town, Punta Arenas (Sandy Point). Originally founded in 1848 as a military and penal colony, this quiet town relies mostly on sheep-farming (sheep that came from the Falkland Islands) and is beginning to expand with tourism. A number of turn-of-the-century buildings remain, including large *palacios* belonging to the town's wealthy families, and some are so luxurious that they are declared *monumentos nacionales.*

Tourist Information

Punta Arenas is laid out on a grid system around the Plaza de Armas (Plaza Muños Gamero). Sernatur is the Chilean government tourist organisation, and its office on Seguel 689, ℂ 241330/225385, is just off the square. There are also tourist kiosks in the centre of the square and at Avenida Colón, block 700.

What to See

A room-by room regional history of early European settlement is laid out in the opulent 19th-century mansion of an wealthy Patagonian sheep-farmer, the **Museo de Historia Regional Braun-Menéndez**, Magellanes 949 (*open Tues–Sat 11am–4pm, Sun 11–1pm*). Original furnishings and an excellent photographic collection make this an atmospheric introduction to the area's history. The town's walled **cemetery**, Avenida Bulnes 949, a 15min walk directly north from the Plaza de Armas, also gives a good intro-duction to the region's history, with the extravagant tombs of the town's illustrious citizens and, by contrast, a monument to the extinct Ona people. The **Instituto de la Patagonia**, Bulnes y Los Flamencos, 4km north of the city centre, ℂ 244216 (*open Mon–Fri 9–12 and 3–6pm; adm*) has outdoor exhibits such as a reconstructed typical settler's house, shearing shed and agricultural machinery. If you haven't had enough of ships yet, the **Naval Museum** is at O'Higgins 989 (*open Mon–Fro 9.30–12.30 and 3–6pm, Sat 10am–1pm and 3–6pm*).

If you have the time, the **Reserva Forestal Magellanes** is a few km west of town along Avenida Independencia and then uphill. There is a self-guided nature trail. Ask at the tourist office for details.

Eating Out

Look out for *centollas*, the crabs which are a regional delicacy: if you can afford it, try them at **Sotitos**, O'Higgins 1138, ℂ 245365 (*expensive*). Many of the city-centre hotels offer good set-price lunches. For atmosphere try **Asturias**, Lautaro Navarro 967, ℂ 243763 (*expensive–moderate*) or **El Mercado**, Mejicana 617, ℂ 247415 (*moderate*).

The Falkland Islands & South Georgia

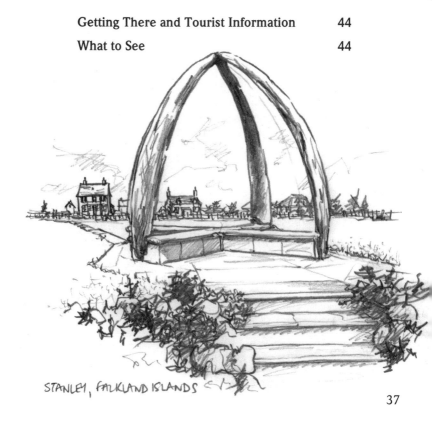

STANLEY, FALKLAND ISLANDS

The Falkland Islands

The Falkland Islands, called the Islas Malvinas in Argentina, consists of two groups of islands in the South Atlantic nearly seven hundred miles north of Antarctica and three hundred miles north east of the tip of South America. The two groups are East Falkland and its surrounding islands, and West Falkland, also with smaller islands. East and West are separated by the Falkland Sound. The two hundred-odd islands cover about 2700 square miles—making the Falklands a little over half the size of Wales, and four times the size of Rhode Island.

The Falkland Islands and South Georgia

There are about 2100 Falklanders at present; they often refer to themselves as kelpers, a name which originated with the seaweed they once harvested in great quantities around the shores of the islands. About 1500 live in the capital, Port Stanley, which is situated on East Falkland. The islanders call the countryside outside Stanley 'the camp'. It is mainly treeless heathland covered with tussock and other low grass. Not for nothing have this landscape and climate often been compared with Scotland.

Average monthly temperatures in the Falklands are lower than in Britain, though it rarely falls below about −1°C, and in summer the Falklands can be very pleasant. Visitors should be aware that it is windy, and dress accordingly.

The Falklands are a British Colony and the Governor is appointed from London. The islands benefited from an injection of funds from London after the conflict and this has been used to improve the infrastructure—there is a vast new school in Stanley, for example, and a large indoor swimming pool. Roads are on the increase.

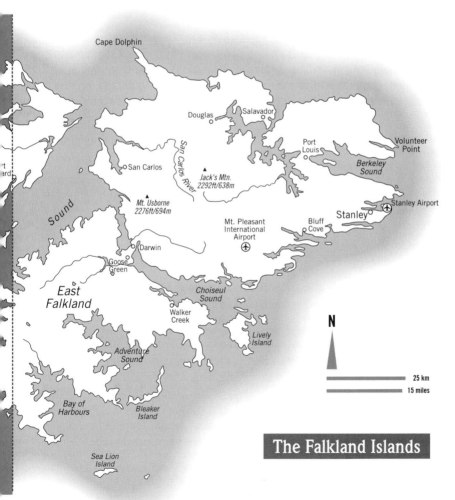

The Falkland Islands

Outside of Stanley, most Falklanders are sheep farmers, and their properties are scattered over the islands. There are well over half a million sheep. Most of the large farms have been subdivided into one-man bands, and the few remaining large holdings, for example at Goose Green, have greatly reduced populations now. Fishing licence fees provide the government with a good income, as do other fishing-related activities. The hot topic in the Falklands at the moment is the looming spectre of oil. Everyone seems to agree that it's there; the question is, is it worth getting it out? In the autumn of 1996 drilling companies submitted tenders for licences, so it's inevitable now that the rigs will be appearing around the Falklands.

History

First sightings are recorded at the end of the 16th century. In 1764 French sailors established a small settlement on the Falklands, and during the remaining years of the 18th century British and Spanish colonists were also present on the islands. The Spanish forced the British out in 1770, but were themselves required to depart in 1771. No ownership was formalized. In 1831 a warship from the United States arrived and booted out some settlers who had arrived from Buenos Aires in 1820. British rule was re-established in 1833. This lasted until 1982, when Argentinian troops returned to claim what they believed to be theirs. The invasion took place on 2 April, and a Task Force was immediately despatched from Britain. When this force finally got to the South Atlantic a short, bloody conflict resulted in the Argentinian command on the Falklands capitulating on 14 June.

Most of the action in the war took place in the north of East Falkland, and so the majority of the land remains just as it was before.

Getting There

The RAF run scheduled TriStar flights twice-weekly between Brize Norton in Oxfordshire and Mount Pleasant on East Falkland, 35 miles from Stanley. It costs about £2300 return for a standard ticket, but group rates and APEX fares are available. The Falklands Islands Tourist Board in London can supply further information (see below). The TriStars refuel in Ascension Island. The Chilean airline AEROVIAS DAP operates a service between Punta Arenas and Stanley weekly during the summer and fortnightly in the winter. The cost is about US $350 one-way.

Getting Around

The best thing to do in the Falklands is lace up your walking boots and hike through the countryside. If you want to cover long distances it is possible to hire a car (though there aren't many available) or a four-wheel drive. Several enterprising kelpers have set themselves up with Land Rovers as tourist guides. The Falklands Islands Government Air Service (FIGAS) offers a limited air taxi service if you want to island-hop. Planes depart from the small airfield at Stanley, not Mount Pleasant.

The Falklands Islands Tourist Board have an office on the main street in Stanley; it is on the public jetty, not far from the cathedral. There is also an information desk at the airport. Otherwise, the tourist board can be contacted in Stanley by telephone on ✆ 22215 or ✆ 22281, or by fax on ✉ 22619. They also have an office in London, at 14 Broadway, Westminster, London SW1H 0BH; ✆ (0171) 222 2542; ✉ 222 2375.

The tourist board offers a guide to Stanley as well as lists of accommodation. Several informative trail leaflets are published locally and can be obtained at the tourist office. Good maps are on sale cheaply. You will be given instruction on how to avoid unexploded mines.

The currency used is the Falklands Island pound, which has the same value as the £ sterling. There is a bank on the main street (Ross Road). British currency can be used everywhere, but the same is not true of the Falklands pound so dispose of your surplus before you leave.

What to See

Wildlife

The wildlife is one of the main attractions of the Falkland Islands. Few sights are more uplifting than the cadmium yellows and sage greens of tussock grass touched by sunshine, undergrowth rustled by the striped wings of a flock of upland geese, a Magellanic penguin peaking out of its burrow in the dunes or a squiggle of steamer ducks at the edge of the aquamarine water, flapping their redundant wings like the paddles of a steamer.

Species of **penguins** include rockhopper, gentoo (especially at Rock Point), and Magellanic, the latter known locally as jackass penguins because of their peculiar braying call. Magellanics are unique among penguins as they burrow in sand dunes. They breed in the Falklands and fly north in the austral winter. A colony of king penguins breeds at Volunteer Point not far from Stanley. You can see Magellanic penguins only a mile or so from Stanley. **Volunteer Point** and its king penguins are ten miles away; the place is a kind of wildlife sanctuary, but it is usually possible to arrange a lift or hire a Land Rover, with or without a driver, if it's too far to walk.

The Falklands are an ornithologist's paradise and every year groups of foreign birders arrive to spend their holidays marching round with binoculars glued to their faces. Ground-nesting **birds** include snipe and upland geese (the famous inn on Stanley's main street was named after this latter bird, which is ubiquitous in the tussock). Some birds have local names: the Falkland Islands flightless steamer duck, for example, is known as a logger, and the giant petrel is called a stinker (if one of these birds vomits near you to warn you off the eggs, you will understand the provenance of this name). Many of the sandy bays are popular feeding grounds for waders, waterfowl and gulls. You can hardly avoid seeing—for example—pied oystercatchers, two-banded plovers and Patagonian crested ducks. Other birds include peregrine falcons, king shags, blackbrowed albatross and black-crowned night herons.

Offshore, various **seals**, **dolphins** and occasionally **whales** can sometimes be seen from the beaches. Southern sea lions breed in the Falklands archipelago between late December and the end of January.

Other Attractions

Some local guides offer the **'82 Tour**, which includes visits to many conflict sites (such as Goose Green and San Carlos). Trout fishing is also available, as is diving (including gear hire). Mount Usborne is a good hiking spot if you want great scenery, and there are many challenging peaks nearby for climbers. This is all in the northern half of East Falkland. If you want to go further afield you'll have to use the air taxi service.

Cruise ships may stop at **Bleaker Island** or **Sea Lion Island**, both of which belong to the East Falkland group, or, in the West Falklands, **New Island**, **Carcass Island** or **West Point**. The scenery and wildlife at all these places is spectacular. Sea Lion Island, for example, which is five miles long and one-and-a-quarter wide, is the home of Magellanic, gentoo and rockhopper penguins, southern elephant seals and forty species of nesting birds. **Port Howard** is an old-style sheep station community on West Falkland, on the east coast.

Keppel Island, next to **Pebble** off the north coast of West Falkland, also has a sheep station. In the mid-19th century Keppel was the home of European missionaries eager to convert canoeing Yahgan Indians from the southern tip of South America. Many ruins of their buildings, and graves, can be seen. **Saunders Island**, which is the next one along, was the site of the first British garrison in the Falklands, in the 18th century. Although the Spanish destroyed most of it, some ruins can be seen.

Stanley

Stanley is a pleasant small town. Most of the houses are built of clapboard with brightly coloured corrugated iron roofs. The streets are often described as reminiscent of Victorian England. It is easy to see why this comparison is made—but the wind of change has blown through Stanley as it has everywhere else. Forces television broadcasts tapes sent from the United Kingdom for about ten hours a day (programmes arrive a fortnight after they have appeared in Britain). Some people have satellite dishes too.

In the past the Falklands attracted **shipwrecks** like iron filings to a magnet, and there are many interesting hulks poking out of the water. The mizzen mast of HMS *Great Britain* lies on the shore on Stanley's main street.

There is a strikingly large **cathedral** on Ross Road, dating from 1892, and next to it is an arch made of whalebones, commemorating the 1933 centenary of British rule.

The **museum** on Ross Road West, ✆ 27428, (*open Tues–Fri 10.30–12 and 2–4, Sun 10–12; adm*) has a charming and extremely well-arranged collection of Falklands history and memorabilia; it is worth making an extra effort to visit. On the coast road not far off you can see the **memorial** to the Battle of the Falklands in 1914 in which Admiral Sturdee routed Admiral von Spee's naval squadron. While at this end of town, have a look at **Government House**, the governor's residence for over a century and an attractive building set in its own manicured lawns.

Where to Stay

Stanley has a wide range of accommodation. The most well known hotel, and the liveliest, is the **Upland Goose** on the front, ✆ 21455. It has two bars and a restaurant. Others include the **Malvina House Hotel**, 3 Ross Road, ✆ 21355, and the **Warrah Guest House**, 46 St John St, ✆ 22649. Various small islands have comfortable lodges, for example Sea Lion Island and Pebble Island. Self-catering cottages are also available on a seasonal basis. If you get a long way off the beaten track you'll probably find a friendly Falkland family who will be happy to put you up for a small charge.

Accommodation changes quickly in the Falklands. For all information, and booking, contact the tourist board.

Eating Out

It's very easy to get a decent meal in Stanley. Just cruise along the main front on foot and take your pick from a three-course meal in the Upland Goose to bar snacks in the numerous pubs. As for nightlife, you'll probably be limited to a bar crawl (though it takes a while to get round all the pubs in Stanley, and by the time you reach the last you won't remember the first). If you are extra lucky you might catch the local group The Pigs playing live at—of course—The Trough.

South Georgia

South Georgia is the second largest of the islands in the vast ocean surrounding Antarctica. It is also the highest, the most mountainous and one of the remotest inhabited spots on the planet. It lies northeast of the tip of the Antarctic Peninsula and southeast of the Falklands and the tip of South America. It is in fact roughly equidistant (932 miles) from Port Stanley and the nearest point of continental Antarctica. South Georgia is roughly crescent-shaped, and it is 105 miles long and between one and eighteen miles wide. A handful of small islets and rocks are scattered around it, notably Bird Island off the northern tip, where the British Antarctic Survey maintain a small scientific station.

The topography of South Georgia is characterized by mountains, fjords, glaciers and lakes. Half the island's surface area is permanently covered with snow and ice, and as a result flora and other vegetation is limited to coastal areas.

There is no indigenous population. The people of South Georgia—often fewer than 30—now consist of members of the garrison domiciled at King Edward Point, and a handful of scientists from the British Antarctic Survey.

Landscape and wildlife are of course the attractions for the visitor; on a clear, sunny day, South Georgia is stupendous.

History

Discovery is disputed, but in all probability the island was first sighted by the London-based merchant Antoine de la Roche in 1675. A century later Captain Cook made the first survey of this isolated territory, when he was searching for the fertile southern continent of popular imagination. He was not enamoured of the place (*see* **History**, p.121). Cook named many features on South Georgia, besides christening the island itself after King George III.

The human history of South Georgia is largely the story of sealing and whaling. Once Cook had published his expedition reports, men began to arrive on South Georgia in search of a fortune. Although many expeditioners, sealers and whalers camped on the island when they needed shelter (some for many months), a permanent population was not established until the whaling station was founded at the sheltered bay of Grytviken in the middle of the outer coast of the crescent in 1904. It was established by the visionary Norwegian whaling captain C.A. Larsen, and in the years that followed five other whaling stations were built on South Georgia. Floating whaling factories also clung to the shore. The population in these years was mainly Norwegian.

The International Polar Year Expedition at South Georgia in 1882–3 brought the first land-based scientists; many have followed. After the demise of whaling in the region, the population shrank. Since 1908, South Georgia has formed part of the Falkland Islands Dependencies, which means that it is governed by Britain. Argentina disputes this sovereignty, and as a result South Georgia was invaded during the 1982 conflict by Argentinian military forces who were removed after three weeks by the Royal Navy.

Since 1909 South Georgia has had its own magistrate, appointed by the Governor of the Falklands. The position is now occupied by the commander of the garrison.

Getting There, and Tourist Information

There is no scheduled air or sea service, and nowhere on the island to stay. Antarctica starts here.

The island uses the Falklands pound, which is on a par with sterling. A very large part of South Georgian revenue is generated by philatelic sales, as the island produces its own stamps. These make excellent souvenirs.

What to See

Wildlife

South Georgia is teeming with life. Broadly speaking you will see the same species here as on the Falklands—but there are more of them. Species range from beetles and flies to the enormous **southern elephant seal**. During the moulting season, at its height in February and March, elephant seals form wallows behind many of the beaches. They lie close

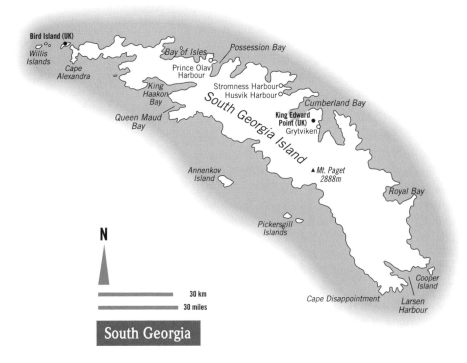

South Georgia

together in the mud and emit a fantastically pungent smell. **Fur seals** have staged a remarkable recovery since they were hunted almost to extinction, and hundreds of thousands breed on South Georgia, mainly on beaches in the north west. The **leopard** and **Weddell seals** are also found, but in lesser numbers.

Although the **whale** population was decimated during the long years of commercial exploitation, if you sail around the Southern Ocean in the vicinity of South Georgia you are likely to see at least a pod of killers.

South Georgia is home to a fascinating variety of **birds**, breeding and non-breeding. The king **penguin** breeds at over thirty sites, but the macaroni penguin is the most numerous: over five million breeding pairs. Gentoos, chinstraps and rockhoppers are also present.

Of the flighted birds, most are of the seabird variety but South Georgia even boasts some freshwater and terrestrial species. These latter include the South Georgia pintail, which is unique to the island. Sheathbills, shags, terns, pipits, teals, petrels and prions can also be seen. The wandering albatross breeds on Bird Island and other outcrops. Other species include the light-mantled sooty albatross, the black-browed and the grey-headed.

Finally, **reindeer** (*Rangifer tarandus*) were introduced by Norwegian whalers in 1909. In fact, three separate consignments of reindeers were brought in for meat and sport, and although they have subsequently flourished, two quite different reindeer populations still exist on South Georgia. The two have not interbred owing to their different geographical habitats. There are probably about two thousand reindeer in total.

Although South Georgia has its own indigenous grasses, herbs and ferns, the botanical landscape is dominated by mosses, lichens and liverwort. In addition, many flowering plants have been introduced and have flourished. Most of these are visible around King Edward Point.

Some of the wildlife mentioned in this chapter is described more fully in **Wildlife**, pp.87–103).

Other Attractions

The **abandoned whaling stations** afford fascinating glimpses of the past, as do the weatherbeaten **sealers' gravestones**—if you can find them. At the main whaling station, in Grytviken, many of the buildings are intact. Founded in 1904 (*see* above), whaling continued at Grytviken until the station closed in 1965. A visit to the **grave of Sir Ernest Shackleton** in Grytviken cemetery is a must. He died in 1922 in the cabin of his ship the *Quest*, which was anchored in King Edward Cove (*see* **History**, pp.130–31, for the story of Shackleton's assault on the unclimbed mountains behind Grytviken after his voyage in the *James Caird* from Elephant Island).

The **church at Grytviken** was the first to be built in the Antarctic. It was actually designed and first used in Norway, and then in 1913 it was dismantled, brought south and erected on South Georgia. It is maintained by the British Antarctic Survey and the Navy, and a service is occasionally held. It is an attractive white Alpine-style building with a steeple, a sharply sloping roof and pretty arched windows.

The **South Georgia Whaling Museum** consists of an excellent collection of artefacts, photographs and memorabilia in the house which once belonged to the manager of the Grytviken Whaling Station. If you are travelling in a group, your tour guide will have arranged entry. For solo travellers, the commander of the garrison at King Edward Point less than a mile away holds the key to the museum. There is a small shop which sells a range of souvenirs, and a walking map of the vicinity is also available.

DRY VALLEYS

Antarctic Sights

The Antarctic Peninsula and Surrounding Regions

The Antarctic Peninsula is the wonky finger of land sticking out of the Antarctic continent in the direction of South America. The peninsula is the most accessible part of the continent, being the least beleaguered with pack ice and enjoying the warmest climate, and it is surrounded by numerous islands and island groups. As a result it is the most popular destination for tourist cruises. It is the site of a large proportion of the Antarctic scientific bases, and its coastline is peppered with islands and bays. Stone hut ruins from Otto Nordenskjöld's expedition are situated at Hope Bay and Paulet Island.

Deception Island

Deception Island is one of the sub-Antarctic South Shetlands off the tip of the peninsula, and a favourite destination for cruise ships. The island is in fact the rim of a volcano, with a small break in the circle, which provides a perfect calm harbour enclosed by towering snow-covered walls. (This opening is called Neptune's Bellows.) The volcano last erupted in 1971, and the landscape is characterised by hard black volcanic ash. Deception was often used as base by sealers and whalers, most recently in 1931, and the disintegrating Whaler's Bay, with its 300m-wide beach is now a popular tourist spot. Many visitors take a dip in the thermal pools at Pendulum Cove, though the water temperatures are rather erratic and can vary wildly within a few metres. This is the perfect photo-opportunity. Deception Island has several large chinstrap penguin colonies; the one at Baily Head has 120,000 pairs.

Drake Passage

Most cruises to Antarctica depart from South America and proceed south via this stretch of water. Here you will cross the Antarctic Convergence where the cold southern waters meet the warmer Atlantic.

The Passage is named after the English navigator and buccaneer Sir Francis Drake (1540–96). Drake was the first Englishman to sail around the world. He also, in 1588, commanded a fleet against the Spanish Armada.

Half Moon Island

A tiny crescent-shaped island, lying off Livingston Island in the South Shetlands, and a very popular cruise destination. The small Argentinian station Teniente Camára is here, as are several thousand chinstrap penguins.

Hope Bay

Another popular destination for tourist ships, Hope Bay is right on the tip of the Antarctic Peninsula and is often the place where visitors first set foot on the continent itself. It has

Laurie Island
Coronation Island
South Orkney Islands

Clarence Island
Arctowski (Poland)
Artigas (Uruguay)
Bellingshausen (Russia)
Teniente Rodolfo Marsh (Chile)
Great Wall (China)
Elephant Island

Joinville Island

King George Is.
Nelson Island
Robert Island
Greenwich Is.
Livingston Is.

South Shetland Islands

Hope Bay
Esperanza (Argentina)
Marambio (Argentina)

James Ross Island

Deception Island
Smith Island

Brabant Island

Anvers Island
Palmer (USA)
Lemaire Channel
Vernadsky (Ukraine)

Larsen Ice
Shelf

Biscoe Islands

Weddell Sea

Adelaide Island
Rothera
(UK)

Palmer Land

Filchner
Shelf

Berkner
Island

Alexander Island

George VI Sound

Wilkins Ice
Shelf

Bellingshausen
Sea

Ronne Ice
Shelf

Vinson Massif (4897m/16,062ft)
Ellsworth Mountains

West Antarctica

Amundsen
Sea

49

the largest colony of Adélie penguins in the world. Visitors can see an old British station and a modern Argentinian one, as well as the ruins of a hut from the Swede Otto Nordenskjöld's expedition.

King George Island

The largest of the South Shetland islands, the archipelago strung out to the north of the peninsula. King George Island is positively bristling with bases, despite being only 10% ice-free. The Chileans are here, as are the Russians, Chinese, Uruguayans, Poles, Argentinians, South Koreans and Brazilians.

Many cruise ships call at King George; cruise companies usually make arrangements in advance for base visits. The Poles at Arctowski station receive the most cruise ship visitors. If you are lucky enough to visit several bases, notice how each one reflects the national characteristics of its inhabitants.

Wildlife on King George Island includes chinstrap penguins and elephant seals.

Lemaire Channel

This features on most Antarctic cruises which visit the peninsular side of the continent, and it must rank as one of the most photogenic places on the planet. Have plenty of film in your pocket when you go out on deck for this. First navigated in 1898, the channel is fairly narrow—it is actually a geologic fault between Booth Island and the Antarctic Peninsula itself—and is lined with steep glaciers and mountains (many unclimbed). Humpback and killer whales often cruise in the Lemaire, and your ship will be able to slow up so you get a good view.

Paradise Harbour

A typically beautiful peninsular landscape embracing bergs, mountains and the red roofs of Chile's Gonzalez Videla base and the Argentinian Almirante Brown.

Paulet Island

In 1903 a team from Otto Nordenskjöld's Swedish expedition were forced to winter on Paulet Island when their ship was crushed in the pack ice of the Weddell Sea. The men lived mainly off penguins and their eggs. This small, volcanic island is situated on the edge of the Weddell Sea, immediately to the east of Dundee and Joinville Islands. It was named after the Rt. Hon. Lord George Paulet, a British navy captain, and was discovered by the James Clark Ross expedition (*see* p. 000). The whole group lies off the northern tip of the Antarctic peninsula. Cruise ships often stop at Paulet, allowing tourists to go ashore in Zodiacs to visit the huge Adélie colony.

Port Lockroy

A natural harbour on Wiencke Island, Port Lockroy serviced whaling factory ships in the early years of this century. In 1943 it was chosen as the site of a British base. The restored main hut of these pioneering Brits, called Bransfield House, was named after the navigator Edward Bransfield, who sailed near the peninsula in 1820 and may have been one of the first men to see Antarctica. Wildlife in the area includes gentoo penguins, blue-eyed shags and crabeater seals, and whalebones are scattered about the beach.

Signy Island

Situated in the South Orkney Group in the northern part of the Weddell Sea, Signy is the site of a summer-only base belonging to the British Antarctic Survey. Signy Station, established in 1947, is a research centre for scientists working on freshwater and terrestrial biology. They are particularly interested in the lakes and streams on the island, and in seal and penguin population biology.

About eight people are based at Signy each season, including support staff. Until 1995 it was a year-round station. The base is not accessible by air. It is resupplied at the end of each summer season by a BAS vessel.

Snow falls on Signy Island on about 280 days a year, and summer temperatures range from zero to 3°C.

The Ross Sea and Around

Owing to its heavy ice cover, the Ross Sea area has only really been accessible to tourists over the last fifteen years, and is still nothing like as busy as the peninsula and the subantarctic islands. However, it offers many rewards, among them the chance to see how the early explorers of the Heroic Age (*see* pp.125–34) made camp and built huts as shelter, the unusual geological formation called the Dry Valleys, and Mount Erebus rising from the horizon on Ross Island.

Cape Adare

This headland is the northernmost gateway to the Ross Sea. As a tourist venue it boasts a huge Adélie penguin colony and the ruins of Carsten Borchgrevink's hut (*see* 'Historic Huts', below). One of Borchegrevink's party, Nikolai Hanson, died on the expedition and was granted his request to be buried on a ridge behind the hut. He was the first man to be buried in Antarctica. Strong climbers can visit his grave, which is marked by an iron cross. On its discovery in 1841, the Cape was named by James Clark Ross after his friend, the MP Viscount Adare.

The Ross Sea and Around

Transantarctic Mountains

Nimrod Glacier

Byrd Glacier

Cook Mountains

Royal Society Range

Dry Valleys

Ross Island

See next page

VICTORIA LAND

Drygalski Ice Tongue

Terra Nova Bay (Italy)

Ross Ice Shelf

Ross Sea

Cape Hallett

Possession Islands

Cape Adare

OATES LAND

GEORGE V LAND

TERRE ADÉLIE

Dumont D'Urville (France)

Mawson's Hut

Commonwealth Bay

South Pole (magnetic) 65°S, 139°E

Dumont D'Urville Sea

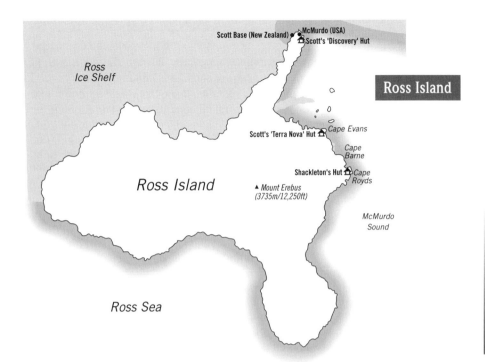

Scott Base (New Zealand)
McMurdo (USA)
Scott's 'Discovery' Hut

Ross
Ice Shelf

Ross Island

Scott's 'Terra Nova' Hut
Cape Evans

Cape
Barne

Shackleton's Hut
Cape
Royds

Ross Island
▲ *Mount Erebus*
(3735m/12,250ft)

McMurdo
Sound

Ross Sea

Cape Evans

Situated on Ross Island, in the lee of Mount Erebus and twelve miles from McMurdo, Cape Evans is the site of Scott's second Hut (*see* 'Historic Huts', below). Next to the hut, on Wind Vane Hill, visitors can easily climb to a cross erected in memory of three men from the Ross Sea Party who died while laying depots for Shackleton during the eventful Imperial Transantarctic Expedition of 1914–17.

Cape Royds

Situated about three miles from Cape Evans along the coast of Ross Island, Royds was chosen as the base for Shackleton's *Nimrod* expedition which set out from Britain in 1907 (*see* 'Historic Huts'). It is also the site of a large Adélie penguin colony.

Commonwealth Bay

This is on the right hand side as you look at a map. The Australasian Antarctic Expedition, led by Douglas Mawson, made its base here between 1912 and 1914. A group of huts still stands (though they are iced up) as does a memorial cross to two men who died on Mawson's epic Far Eastern Sledging Journey.

The French Dumont d'Urville station is in the region.

Dry Valleys

This series of arid, sculpted valleys runs off the Antarctic continent opposite Ross Island, and was created by the advances and retreats of glaciers through the Transantarctic Mountains (see **Ice and Science**, p.64). They are sometimes visited by helicopter from cruise ships stationed in the Ross Sea. No rain has fallen in the Dry Valleys for two million years, and much of the rock surface is exposed. The three main valleys, first discovered in 1903, are Victoria, Wright and Taylor.

Historic Huts

These atmospheric glimpses of the past feature on some cruise itineraries and are well worth a visit. They are the wooden and stone expedition bases of Antarctic expeditions at the beginning of the century, quite literally frozen in time. The star attraction is **Captain Scott's hut** from his 1910–13 *Terra Nova* expedition, situated at Cape Evans on Ross Island. Your tour guide will have arranged to have the key to the hut, and will explain the conditions of entry—the New Zealand Antarctic Heritage Trust maintains these huts in good condition (although the cold preserves them, the wind can do a lot of damage) and it is important to respect their requests. Only a certain number of people should enter the huts at any one time (twelve at Cape Evans), and you should brush as much snow as possible from your boots when you enter. Salt particles hasten the corrosion of metal objects so you should remove any clothing wet from sea water and any sea-ice crystals from your boots. Do not handle any items.

The **'Discovery Hut'** is also situated on Ross Island. This was built on a spur by Captain Scott's 1901–4 National Antarctic Expedition, and now overlooks McMurdo station. It served primarily as a storage area, laboratory and handy stage set for the makeshift theatrical extravaganzas put on by the crew, who lived alongside on board the *Discovery*. The hut was also used as an advance base for sledging operations for later expeditions.

Further along the spur, Vince's Cross still stands as a memorial to a seaman from the *Discovery* expedition who fell over an ice cliff during a blizzard.

The third major hut on Ross Island is **Shackleton's** at Cape Royds. This was used as a base by the *Nimrod* team in 1907–9, led by Ernest Shackleton. Note the glass jars of table salt stored in boxes alongside the hut, and the spokes of the motor vehicles Shackleton took south (the first ever seen in Antarctica).

It is also possible to visit the Australian **Sir Douglas Mawson's hut** at Commonwealth Bay in George V Land. It was built as a base on his 1911–14 expedition. At Cape Adare you can see the hut from Carsten Borchgrevink's 1898–1900 *Southern Cross* expedition. The dilapidated remains of the entrance porch from a hut erected by a sledging party from Scott's *Terra Nova* expedition are also at Cape Adare.

If you want to take photographs inside the huts—and they are extraordinarily photo-genic—keep the batteries in your flash unit in your mitten or a warm breast pocket until

ABOVE: *An ice cave within the Erebus Glacier Tongue.*

RIGHT: *Pack ice off the coast of the Peninsula.*

ABOVE: *McMurdo base (USA)*.

LEFT (TOP TO BOTTOM):
- *A weatherhaven protecting science equipment on Lake Hoare in the Dry Valleys.*
- *An icebreaker crew play ball on frozen McMurdo Sound.*
- *A mummified seal, dead for 100 years. Antarctica knows no decay.*
- *Geodesic dome at the American base at the South Pole.*
- *Terra Nova Bay, the Italian Antarctic base.*

BELOW: *Staff at the American base reflected in the globe marking 90°S.*

ABOVE: *Battleship Promontory, one of the few spots in Antarctica not permanently covered in ice. A paradise for geologists.*

RIGHT: *The ski of a twin otter plane.*

BELOW: *Another hectic day in Antarctica.*

View from Linnaeus Terrace
in the Transantarctic Mountains.

you need them; the huts are as cold inside as out. Tripods can get in other people's way in a confined space, and also run the risk of damaging delicate artefacts; it's probably advisable not to use one unless you have a lot of time at Cape Evans and can enter the hut again after each group has had its turn. It's more important to absorb the atmosphere anyway.

It is worth taking a torch along in your pocket when you visit the huts (again, keep the batteries warm) as even a small beam will illuminate the dark corners. The photographer Herbert Ponting's dark room, for example, at the far end (away from the door) of the Cape Evans hut is a wondrous cubbyhole, but you won't be able to see anything without a bit of light. If you don't have a torch don't worry: your tour guide will probably have one.

Don't forget to look at the outbuildings and paraphernalia outside the main body of the huts. At Cape Evans there is an anchor and ski runners, and at Cape Royds a dog house complete with frozen dog.

McMurdo Station

The largest Antarctic base, situated on Ross Island, McMurdo is the hub of the American Antarctic Program. It was established in 1956 and has grown from a handful of huts to a complex logistical centre of more than a hundred buildings and three landing sites for Hercules aircraft arriving from New Zealand. The winter population, consisting almost exclusively of support staff, numbers approximately 250, and during the summer season as many as 1300 people are based at McMurdo, many of them scientists in transit to field camps.

The station was named after Archibald McMurdo, first lieutenant of the *Terror*, one of the ships James Clark Ross took south in his pioneering 1839–43 expedition (*see* **Geopolitics**, pp.114–5, for more information on America in Antarctica).

Mount Erebus

The Eiffel Tower of Antarctica (*see also* 'Ross Island'). This 12,444ft (3795m) active volcano was first climbed in 1908 by a party from Shackleton's *Nimrod* expedition, and 71 years later it was the scene of a horrific air crash when a New Zealand tourist plane flew into the lower slopes, killing all 257 people aboard.

Ross Ice Shelf

Roughly 520,000 sq km in size, and up to 1000m thick, this is the largest of the many ice shelves surrounding the jagged coastline. They are formed when the layer of ice on the surface of Antarctica reaches the edge of the land and tips over into the ocean; they are literally great shelves of floating ice 'glued' to land on one or more sides (*see also* **Ice and Science**, p. 000). In 1841, James Clark Ross was the first to see the ice shelf which now bears his name; he called it a 'barrier', a name which was adopted by later explorers, because it was blocking the way to the Pole.

This is what the great navigator wrote in his diary when he discovered this vast ice shelf.

'But this extraordinary barrier of ice, of probably more than a thousand feet in thickness, crushes the undulations of the waves, and disregards their violence; it is a mighty and wonderful object, far beyond anything we could have thought or conceived.'

Ross Island

The highlight of cruises starting from New Zealand and also of circumnavigations, Ross Island is partially surrounded by the Ross Ice Shelf and separated from the Antarctic continent by McMurdo Sound. The interior of the island is hilly and dominated by two volcanoes, Mounts Erebus and the smaller Terror, named after the ships in which James Clark Ross sailed south in the 1840s. It is the site of three of the most significant historic huts as well as McMurdo, the largest base in Antarctica. Scott Base, the only New Zealand station, is located just over the hill from McMurdo near a spot called Butter Point. Next to McMurdo sturdy visitors can climb Observation Hill to inspect the cross erected by Scott's men just before they left at the end of the *Terra Nova* expedition. It is made of Australian jarrah wood and inscribed with a line from Tennyson's *Ulysses*: 'To strive, to seek, to find, and not to yield.'

Terra Nova Bay

The site of the only Italian base in Antarctica, Terra Nova Bay is situated in northern Victoria Land on the coast of the Northern Foothills. The bay is overlooked by a spectacular volcano named Mount Melbourne by early British explorers. Terra Nova is a sophisticated summer-only station painted Siena orange and Prussian blue, and the buildings are on stilts. Approximately 50 Italian scientists and support staff are based there each summer (*see* **Geopolitics**, pp.111–12, for more information on the Italian programme). Look out for the graffiti on the wall of the *pinguinatolo*, a recreational hut behind the main base. It is a unique historical record of the human presence at Terra Nova Bay...

DRILLING FOR ICE-DEPTH

Ice and Science

On a map, the Antarctic continent looks like an amorphous blob, its only distinguishing feature a finger tapering off north towards South America. The continent constitutes one tenth of the earth's land surface, and is considerably larger than Europe and one and a half times the size of the United States. It is *fifty* times larger than Great Britain.

More than 99 per cent of this landmass is permanently covered with ice formed by thousands of years of tightly compacted snowfall. (The latest figure from the British Antarctic Survey/Scott Polar Research Institute satellite map reveals a percentage of 99.6.)

The other 0.4 per cent consists of exposed rock. Ninety per cent of the world's ice is in Antarctica, and at its deepest it is well over a mile thick. In places, this ice layer has pushed the land under it far below sea level. The layer of ice on the surface of Antarctica gradually makes its way towards the coast, where it either turns into a floating ice shelf or collapses into the Southern Ocean. As a result, ice shelves surround the jagged coastline; the Ross Ice Shelf is larger than France. Thousands of cubic miles of ice break off the Antarctic coast each year.

The continent consists, broadly speaking, of two **geological zones** divided by the Transantarctic mountain chain. Greater Antarctica (also known as East Antarctica) is generally thought to be one stable plate. Lesser Antarctica (or West), on the other hand, consists of a lot of smaller, unstable plates.

Besides the Transantarctics slicing down the middle, mountains form a ring around much of the continent. Beyond these coastal mountains, in the interior of the continent specific topography tends to disappear into thousands of miles of apparently flat ice. In reality, mountain ranges as high as the Appalachians or the Alps are hiding under this flat ice. The South Pole, the lower axis of the earth's rotation, is located in Greater Antarctica, on the polar plateau. The Pole is also known as the **Geographic South Pole** to distinguish it from the **South Magnetic Pole**, which is the south pole of the earth's magnetic field. The Magnetic Pole moves around steadily, whereas the geographic one remains at ninety degrees south. While the geographic pole is a stable point on the earth, however, the ice lying on top of that earth is moving, so the marker at the South Pole has to be moved a few yards each year to compensate for ice drift.

So Antarctica is an extremely elevated continent. It's just that in the middle at least it looks flat, as the mountains are covered with ice. The mean altitude of the continent is 7500ft, and at its highest the plateau is over 13,000ft (3950m). The highest point in Antarctica is the Vinson Massif in the Ellsworth Mountains: its 17,700ft (5395m) peak makes it a much sought-after destination for top climbers seeking to bag the highest mountain on all the continents.

When a high bit of earth is covered with an especially thick bit of ice, the surface of the continent is high enough to make breathing difficult for the visitor. Being at the South Pole is like being on the summit of a medium-sized mountain. The altitude there is 9300ft (2835m)—one-third of the height of Mount Everest. As a result, a significant percentage of visitors get altitude sickness when they reach the Pole. This doesn't happen to the few hardy types who pull their sledges from the coast, however, as they have had time to acclimatize, but it does afflict some scientists who fly straight in from McMurdo, which is virtually at sea level (the base at the South Pole is American). In addition, the earth's atmosphere is at its most shallow at the North and South Poles. The combination of altitude and shallow atmosphere means that at the Pole the human body receives only about fifty per cent of its normal oxygen supply.

There are **islands** scattered all around the continent. The ones furthest to the north are called sub-Antarctic islands. As many of these islands are further north than the continent itself, some of them are not covered with ice all year round, and most also enjoy a milder climate. The most well-known are the islands off the west of the peninsula, notably the South Shetlands (named by Scottish sealers) which include King George Island. Other archipelagos in the vicinity include the South Orkneys and South Sandwich Islands. Some islands (though none of the South Shetlands) are joined to the Antarctic continent by permanent ice, and others are joined by pack ice most of the time, the exception being mild summers, when they are separated by open water.

Kerguélen is the largest sub-Antarctic island. South Georgia, the second largest, is an occasionally fog-bound chain of mountains which, from the 18th century to the middle of this one, provided a base for sealers and whalers. It is the natural home of an unusually large number of birds and so the focus of ornithological research (*see* **The Falklands and South Georgia**).

Climate and Seasons

For most of the year, central Antarctica enjoys **total darkness** or **total daylight**. The cusps between the two are short and exciting: it might be eight weeks from the moment the sun makes its first appearance over the horizon to the day it never sets. The summer runs from October to late February, and during this period Antarctica is light all the time. The dark winter lasts longer in the interior than on the coast, and the peninsula, being further north than anywhere else on the continent, enjoys the longest summer.

Similarly, Antarctica gets **colder** as you get further in. Coastal bases enjoy a milder climate—indeed, some have a mean summer temperature above freezing. Rothera Station on the peninsula is ten degrees further north than McMurdo on Ross Island. At McMurdo the mean temperature in January is −3°C, whereas at Rothera it is 2°C. At the Pole, the January mean is −28° and the warmest it has ever got is −14°C. It can reach −50° at McMurdo in the winter, but the lowest temperature ever recorded at Rothera is −39°. The coldest time of year everywhere is often early September when the night, like a tide, is in retreat. The chilliest base of all is Vostok, the Russian station high up in the heart of East Antarctica. There scientists have recorded the lowest air temperature in the world, a glacial −129.3°F, which is −89.2°C. The annual mean temperature at Vostok is −55°C— five degrees colder than the South Pole. Besides being so remote, Vostok cannot be adequately supplied by air, and therefore each summer a convoy of heavily laden Kharkovchanka tractors sets out from Mirny, the Russian station on the east coast, carrying food and other essentials for the Vostok workers.

Extremely high **winds**, common all over Antarctica and terrifyingly swift to arrive, can freeze exposed flesh in seconds. That, effectively, is what constitutes frostbite, not initially a highly dangerous injury but one that can soon become fatal, if untreated. The most powerful winds are the ones that rush down off the polar plateau, called katabatic winds. The average wind speed at McMurdo is twelve knots, but winds have exceeded 100 knots. Some places in Antarctica are the windiest in the world—at Port Martin, for example, the annual mean wind speed is almost gale force.

The answer to the popular question, 'How cold is it?' depends on the **wind chill factor**. This is calculated by measuring wind speed and ambient air temperature at the same time. A wind racing along at 35 miles per hour (56 knots), which is fairly usual, reduces an actual temperature of –6°C to –28°C. *See* p.23 for a table showing how the wind chill factor is calculated.

During the polar night the **southern lights** can sometimes be observed in the sky—great fanning displays of colour. The technical name for them is *Aurora australis*, the southern counterpart of the *Aurora borealis*, the northern lights. Both are caused by charged particles from the sun which come whizzing into the earth's atmosphere in the direction of the magnetic poles and hit molecules of gas. The interaction of these solar particles and the earth's magnetic field causes electrical storms which appear as panoplies of colours in the night sky. The auroras which can be observed in the southern sky during the winter yield information about the earth's magnetic field which is valuable to astronomers.

The cold atmosphere means that specialized **meteorological phenomena** can be seen more clearly in Antarctica than elsewhere, especially when it is extra-cold. **Sundogs**, for example, are bright spots in the sky near the sun caused by the diffraction of light by ice crystals in the atmosphere. They are also called parhelion, and they can appear all year round. Other 'halo phenomena' take the form of pillars or arcs. A heavy purply black blanket above the bright band of light on the horizon is caused by the reflection of open water in the lower cloud layer. It is called **ice blink**. You are also likely to see **diamond dust** floating in the air in Antarctica. It looks just like it sounds—sparkling icing sugar which drifts on the breeze. In fact this is simply ice crystallizing in clear air and reflecting the sunlight.

One of the most distinctive features of the Antarctic climate is the clarity of the air. Compared with what we are familiar with at home there is no pollution in the south. On a clear day you can see mountains 60 miles away, and this makes it very hard to assess distance. People are always setting out to walk or ski to a landmark which seems near, but in fact is miles away. The sun can also pose a problem to the Antarctic traveller as the snow surface reflects over 90 per cent of the sunlight falling on it, thus nearly doubling exposure to solar radiation. If you are visiting Antarctica it is important to wear sunblock at all times (*see* **Practical A–Z**, p.26).

The influence of the sea and the typical passage of depressions means that there are more **clouds** above coastal areas and fewer in the interior. In other words, the further a station is inland, the less cloudy its weather. The British station Signy has an average cloud cover of 86 per cent, for example, whereas the South Pole has an average of 41 per cent.

Depressions cannot penetrate very far into the interior of the continent, which means that on the polar plateau there is virtually no **precipitation**. One scientific study puts the annual rainfall of inland Antarctica at less than two inches a year—about the same as the Sahara.

Global Warming (Climatic Change)

Global warming is a phrase which has entered most living rooms via the television set and it certainly presses media buttons. Antarctica holds the key, or one of them, to an understanding of global warming. The regional climate on the peninsula, always the warmest part of Antarctica, has heated up by 2.5°C since the 1940s, and this has weakened the ice shelves—to the extent that in 50 years more than 3000 square miles (7770 sq km) of them have disappeared without being renewed. In 1995 a piece of ice the size of a minor English county broke off the Larsen Ice Shelf and was heading purposefully for the Falklands (in the end it got stuck on an island in the Southern Ocean long before reaching them). In 1967 a 3000-square-mile berg subsequently named Trolltunga snapped off Antarctica at about twelve o'clock on the map. The world record holder measured over 12,000 square miles (31,080 sq km).

Whenever an especially large berg snaps off Antarctica, a raft of catastrophe stories appear in the media about London and New York being flooded by the tide of melted glacier water pouring off Antarctica. The formation of a berg, however—even a particularly huge one—is part of the natural cycle of renewal, and not therefore necessarily indicative of imminent global catastrophe. It is the gradual disintegration of the ice shelves year-on-year which is a new phenomenon, and one which is gripping glaciologists. Since 1990, for instance, the ice which formerly occupied Prince Gustav Channel and connected James Ross Island to the Antarctic Peninsula has crumbled away, and not long before that the Wordie Ice Shelf on the west coast broke up. In early 1997 a fissure opened up in the Larsen Ice Shelf.

Even the gradual disintegration of the ice shelves won't necessarily raise sea levels, though, as, according to the Archimedes Principle, floating ice displaces its own mass of water. If, however, the crumbling of the ice shelves causes the ice sheet lying over the land to discharge more ice, then sea levels will rise. Even in that situation, the extra discharge would have to occur off large areas of the coast, not just the peninsula, before the rest of the planet were to be significantly affected. In other words, it seems unlikely that in our lifetime or that of our children we shall be flooded by ice-cold water as a result of a dramatic rise in global temperatures.

Science

Antarctica is a unique and relatively little known area, to a certain extent a perfect natural laboratory, and it is not surprising that many, many scientists clamour to spend field seasons there. This is a highly competitive arena, as effectively it is not economically possible for any science team to work in the south unless it is selected, and therefore supported, by a government programme. No university could afford, or have the logistical wherewithal, to send its research department to Antarctica.

Some national programmes, such as the American one, take science teams from a wide variety of external institutions, notably universities. In these cases scientists are required to submit proposals a long time in advance of their projected visit. Other programmes, such as the British Antarctic Survey, use in-house scientists permanently employed by the programme who work in laboratories at home, visiting Antarctica once every couple of years. Typically, a scientist might make four or five field visits in the course of a career, but some veterans have been going south every year since the sixties. A field season lasts anything from a month to three months. Very few scientists spend the winter on the continent, simply because there aren't many experiments you can do in total darkness and such low temperatures. Some types of equipment are left running during the winter and maintained by wintering technicians, for example certain telescopes.

There is a heartening degree of international co-operation among the scientific community. All countries operational in Antarctica are required to submit details of their science projects to an international body in order to facilitate the sharing of information. Often countries group together for the really expensive projects (though all Antarctic science is expensive). Cape Roberts, in Victoria Land, for example, is currently the site of one of the most ambitious co-operative projects ever conceived in Antarctica. To investigate the late Cretaceous to mid-Cenozoic history of the Ross Sea region, geologists from five countries are drilling offshore rock cores which will (the scientists hope) yield information on millions of years of tectonic and climatic change.

Biological Sciences (Life Sciences)

Marine biologists have been visiting Antarctica for several decades to investigate the role of phytoplankton, krill, fish and squid in the ecosystem of the Southern Ocean. This became more of a priority in the late seventies in response to growing concern over fish stocks. One of the aims of this branch of marine biology is to determine sustainable harvesting limits. Most of the work has taken place under the wing of the international BIOMASS programme (Biological Investigation of Marine Antarctic Systems and Stocks).

Although it looks on a map as if it is a continuation of the Atlantic and the Pacific, the circumpolar Southern Ocean has a distinct physical boundary marked by the **Antarctic Convergence**. This latter is a complex and turbulent area where cold Antarctic water meets and sinks below the warmer waters of surrounding oceans, resulting in a rapid temperature change of two or three degrees in the surface water (*see* also **Wildlife**, p.99). The Antarctic Convergence is an important boundary for many of the animals and plants that have adapted to Antarctic waters.

Marine biologists have discovered that there is a plant in the ocean that manufactures its own sunscreen. It is a species of **phytoplankton** or alga, an essential and prolific component at the base of the food chain. This particular kind, *Phaeocystis*, blooms near the surface of the ocean when the sea ice is melting, which is also the time when the ozone hole develops. Thus the alga is exposed to relatively high levels of ultraviolet radiation. In clear water, this can damage it to depths of sixty feet. As a result, its survival appears to have depended on coming up with a solution for itself. Similar species elsewhere in the world also have sunscreening substances, but they are at much lower concentrations.

Obviously **ships** are the most appropriate environment for many projects in marine biology and oceanography, and scientists in the field often spend several months 'cruising' the Southern Ocean in an ice-strengthened ship or proper icebreaker fitted with laboratories and sophisticated oceanographical equipment. This includes instruments which can be lowered to a depth of four miles and which use advanced electronics to measure salinity, temperature, current-velocity and so on. Data is transmitted through a conducting cable to a shipboard computer display.

Shipboard biologists are particularly interested in **krill stocks**. The depletion of baleen whales in the Southern Ocean as a result of commercial exploitation has meant the availability of more krill for some of the seals and seabirds—in other words, the ecosystem is responding to disturbance. Scientists want to find more details so that management plans can be produced to preserve the ecosystem for the future. Commercial exploitation of krill itself must only proceed in the knowledge of the consequences. This is the thrust of much of the marine biological research in Antarctica.

All aspects of **penguin behaviour** are studied, though in the case of the emperors special permits are required to access most of the colonies. Scientists researching the life cycle of the emperor have to deal with particular difficulties as a lot of the important bits, such as incubation of the eggs, are conducted in total darkness. One of the leading practitioners in this highly specialized field used to hitch a lift in the annual American supply plane which dropped crates on to the ice in the middle of winter. (This has now been stopped, owing to budget cuts.) At least then this resourceful scientist could get a good look at some of the colonies and see what the birds were up to. The Adélies are easier to deal with. A joint Australian/Italian Adélie programme has achieved considerable success, working largely out of the colony at Edmondson Point near Terra Nova Bay. At Cape Bird on Ross Island, penguin biologists from New Zealand have established an electronic weighbridge which the birds waddle over on their way to the sea.

Research on **seabirds** tends to be grouped around two main questions. First, what is the role of seabirds as predators of Antarctic marine resources, especially krill? Secondly, how are reproductive behaviour and survival affected by age, experience and mate quality?

Seal tagging has been going on for some years in the McMurdo area and elsewhere and it has yielded insights into the population dynamics of the Weddell seal. Similarly, British scientists have been collecting population data on elephant seals on South Georgia and comparing them with similar information gathered during the fifties, when the males were exploited for blubber oil. In addition, elephant seal behaviour is studied to examine details of social organization. Behavioural research into fur seals has investigated the effects of different levels of population density in the rapidly expanding community. Current studies of fur seals deal principally with their diet and its impact on food resources, as well as their behaviour at sea (remote recording devices are used for this).

It is possible to go fishing in Antarctica, though it is not as straightforward as sitting on a riverbank with a rod and a packet of sandwiches. **Fish** scientists spend weeks crouching in small wooden huts on the sea ice. They drill holes in the ice and, using a battery-operated winch positioned over the holes, lower bait 1500ft into the spectral depths. The bait usually consists of fish brought in from New Zealand. If the scientists are lucky, they haul up primeval creatures which survive the depths of the Southern Ocean by producing their own antifreeze. This is how the fish have adapted. Salty sea water doesn't freeze until it reaches −1.8°C, and at this temperature the body fluids of 'normal' fish would freeze. The Antarctic creatures in question have special antifreeze proteins which act like antibodies to ice crystals, wrapping them up as they form so they can't grow. This antifreeze could have commercial potential: aircraft manufacturers, for example, want to see if it can be used to develop a product to prevent aeroplane wings from freezing.

You can, actually, also eat these fish. Antarctic cod has been served up at the McMurdo Thanksgiving dinner and eaten with mashed potato and tinned veg. The fish tend to be very oily, but if you choose carefully which part you eat, you can end up with a tasty plate of sashimi.

Some marine biology is conducted with the assistance of **divers**. Carrying full scuba gear and wearing drysuits specially adapted for extra-cold temperatures, they usually enter the water though holes cut in the ice with a chainsaw. Diving in Antarctic waters is especially dangerous, as divers cannot ascend simply anywhere if they get into difficulties; they have to find the ice hole through which they entered the water.

Wetsuit—Drysuit?

Just as you get wet wearing a wetsuit, with a drysuit you stay dry—an important consideration when the temperature of the water is below freezing. A wetsuit traps water between itself and your skin. A drysuit traps air.

Air conducts heat relatively poorly. Drysuits work by providing insulation with a layer of air. They are the warmest exposure protection, essential under the ice and always used in the rest of the world in water colder than 10°C. Since drysuits are filled with a layer of air, the pressure in them must be equalized as the diver descends. Most suits have specialized inflation/deflation valves for this. Drysuits used in Antarctica are designed to be worn with special thermal undergarments.

Many scientists work on the **partially frozen lakes** in a series of arid valleys which run off the Antarctic continent opposite Ross Island. It has not rained there for two million years. These Dry Valleys were created by the advances and retreats of glaciers through the Transantarctic mountains. Free of ice for about four million years, the valleys are dotted with partially frozen saltwater basins and form one of the most extreme deserts in the world. Some ponds are so saline that they won't freeze even at −60°C, and the water is like molasses. On others, the ice crusts, like lenses, concentrate so much solar energy that the bottom layers can reach temperatures of 25°C above freezing.

The pristine environment of the Dry Valleys attracts scientists from a range of disciplines from coastal ecology to marine biology and geochemistry. These lakes are unique all the way from the ice on the top to the plankton at the bottom. They were formed about 1200 years ago by meltwater from glaciers and some are covered with lids of ice that might be 15ft thick. Usually it is the 50-odd feet of water underneath the ice which interests the scientists, as the permanent ice lid facilitates a uniquely stable water column. Typically, they place instruments in the lake and suck up water from the bottom for analysis. When it come up it is so full of sulphides that it smells of rotten eggs. Sometimes scientists leave their instruments under the ice all winter, the hydraulically fired syringes busily collecting water samples which are retrieved when the team returns the following summer.

Looking under these lakes is literally like going back in time, and the water samples reveal a microbial wonderland. Bacteriologists use them, for example, to study photosynthesis cycles. In particular the lakes have yielded crucial data on nitrates, the single biggest cause of coastal erosion and pollution in the northern hemisphere. Oceans do have an assimilative capacity for nitrates, but they should not be introduced beyond that capacity. Many areas of the world are already a long way beyond their limit.

There are still many questions unanswered in the Dry Valleys. Some of the lakes are frozen all the way down to the bottom, though nobody knows why. Progress is being made, but it is slow, not least because it is a difficult environment for the scientist. Even in the summer, researchers on these lakes are engaged in a constant battle against the big freeze. This is a leitmotif of all Antarctic science. The issue of how to melt holes in the ice lid of the lakes, for example, is an extremely vexing one. Copper coils carrying heated glycol are often used, as well as a range of hand drills. Any scientist who has worked in the south will tell you, however, that whatever instruments you use will freeze, and that Antarctic science teaches you to improvise. Veterans are great subscribers to the conspiracy theory, in that however well an instrument is working when you pack it carefully in its case at home, when you unpack it in the field in Antarctica it will immediately go on strike.

As far as **terrestrial biology** is concerned, most work is conducted on sub-Antarctic islands. These places have been important commercially for more than 200 years and the human influence on the environment is a subject which has exercised the minds of many scientists. Land-based sealing and whaling, for example, which stopped for good in the sixties, left settlements and processing stations to rot. The effects of widespread destruction of the vegetation are still being felt, and it is up to scientists to assess them and produce strategies of damage-limitation. In addition, whalers and sealers introduced domestic animals such as sheep and goats, as well as (by accident) mice and rats, and this has had an adverse effect on the indigenous wildlife and vegetation. The most destructive creatures were the rabbits brought to Kerguélen and Macquarie Island (and still there), and the rats which have proliferated on half the islands. Scientists are looking at ways of reversing the damage that has been caused. The need for conservation is keenly felt.

Australian biologists have been studying the ecology of the **mosses and lichens** on the Windmill Islands, near Casey station. This includes looking at the effects of environmental pollution, for example from alkaline cement dust, on the growth and physiology of the flora.

Atmospheric and Space Physics

Weather patterns are carefully monitored at all bases so scientists can learn more about how Antarctica functions and how its meteorological patterns affect the rest of the world. Surface temperature is recorded, as well as humidity, hours of sunshine, air pressure, wind speed and wind direction. Automatic instruments take care of most of this, though base personnel have to assess visibility and the amount, type and height of clouds. This job is called 'doing the weather', and everyone at camp takes it in turns. When a white-out closes in, doing the weather can be a very unpopular task, although at least under these circumstances it doesn't take long as there certainly won't be any visible cloud.

Scientists at some stations regularly launch **weather balloons** to capture atmospheric data which is then transmitted direct from the balloon back to the home institution or to a computer on base. Balloons sent up from the British station Halley are sometimes equipped with special instruments to capture data from the troposphere, the lower part of the atmosphere where weather systems are active. At the South Pole, balloons are sent up twice a day. They are made from a thin, translucent fabric and carry their instruments in a styrofoam box suspended at the bottom. Usually these balloons are filled with hydrogen, and as they ascend they expand. When they can no longer hold the pressure within them, they burst and come tumbling back to earth. If the on-board instrumentation is sufficiently valuable, a rescue team may be sent out to recover it after it has fallen to earth.

Some manually released balloons reach diameters in excess of ten feet, and the large ones, which go up from a specially built launch pad, measure hundreds of feet. Working with these latter is among the most stressful branches of Antarctic science as the launch is entirely contingent on weather conditions. This can be very frustrating if you have spent three years building a balloon's payload and assembling all the instrumentation, and then you are stuck on base in a white-out watching the season tick away.

Data from the instruments on the balloons is expressed in numeric code and sent via geostationary satellites to meteorological centres in the northern hemisphere where they are collated. It is possible that the weather forecast you watch on television in your living room may have been influenced by Antarctic data. In particular, Antarctic weathermen have attempted to define the role of the Southern Ocean in circulating all of the world's oceans and transferring heat, and their results are included in global models for predicting climatic change.

Antarctica is a natural laboratory for measuring **global pollution** and changes in concentrations of atmospheric gases. For example, scientists have determined how the Southern Ocean and its biological components fix the greenhouse gas carbon dioxide. Using the latest technology, scientists can also view energetic particles from space, or **cosmic rays**, in a manner which cannot be duplicated elsewhere on the globe. They can measure the changes in the atmosphere from the ground to the upper limits with emphasis on the ozone region. It is this last subject—**ozone** detection, or rather, detection of depletion in the ozone layer—that has hit the headlines over the last decade more than any other area of Antarctic scientific research.

Ozone concentrations have been recorded at the British station Halley and the former British station Faraday for over 35 years using an ultraviolet spectrophotometer. The measurements began to show a seasonal decrease, or hole, appearing in the ozone layer over Antarctica each spring. Because the ozone layer protects the earth from harmful ultraviolet radiation, this discovery had serious implications. Antarctic scientists from Britain first brought the devastating news to the world's attention in 1985. It turned out that chlorofluorocarbons (CFCs) released from our aerosol cans and fridges are diffusing into the stratosphere, being broken down and releasing chlorine. When the stratosphere over Antarctica becomes very cold (during the winter), thin clouds form and alter the balance between chlorine and other gases. Then, when the sun comes back, chlorine joins in with the complex catalytic reactions which destroy the ozone layer. When the stratosphere warms up again later in the summer, this process ceases and the ozone concentration increases.

So next time you use a pump action spray, remember that the product exists as a result of the endeavours of scientists battling it out in the icy south.

The **South Pole** offers the sky-scientist excellent viewing conditions. If you want to study the sun in summer, say, from the Pole, it will neither rise nor set, but circle 24 hours a day at a constant elevation. This means you can track it though a dry atmosphere with a consistent thickness. It is remote from most human-generated atmospheric and electro-magnetic disturbance, and usually has clear weather. In addition, it is near the southern ends of the earth's magnetic lines of force, a region in which solar wind particles can directly enter the earth's atmosphere. At the Pole astronomers study gamma rays and other high-energy radiation from space. The National Science Foundation, which runs the American Antarctic Program, has invested a good deal in building up their astronomical work at the Pole.

One of the major projects currently running at the Pole is the ASTRO telescope. The acronym stands for Antarctic Submillimetre Telescope/Remote Observatory. The US-built telescope, which weighs ten tons and can look into distant galaxies, detects short wave-lengths known as **submillimetre radiation**. A team of scientists from North America work at the Pole on the ASTRO project each summer and one person remains to take care of it during the winter, transmitting data to the home institutions. One of ASTRO's notable recent successes was the first detection of atomic carbon in the Magellanic Clouds.

Glaciology

You might be under the illusion that ice is ice—that it's the same as the cubes you put in your drinks. This could not be further from the truth, and nowhere is it more apparent than Antarctica, where there are many different kinds of ice, each one yielding a vastly different array of secrets to the patient glaciologist.

Sea ice, for example, is the stuff that forms on the surface of the Southern Ocean at the onset of winter. It begins as a film ('grease ice'), proceeds through a multitude of stages (bergy bits, growlers, pancake and so on) and, as the temperature drops, spreads and encir-cles the continent. Eventually it forms one solid, floating layer which can reach a thickness of many feet. The growth and decay of Antarctic sea ice is the greatest seasonal event on earth, in terms of mass and energy. Sea ice melts in summer, yet during winter it can cover an area almost as large as the continent itself, which is why you can't get in by ship for half the year. The melting of the sea ice has a profound effect on the environment, and scientists have been researching this for several decades.

Pack ice is the stuff which jostles on the surface of the ocean all the way round Antarctica. It is fragmented into floes which crash into each other. The pack remains all year round, though it increases its surface area several times over in the winter. When ocean currents push up warmer water, large ice-free areas appear in the pack, and ships can slip through them. Problems arise when the pack then suddenly closes, trapping the ship like a vice. Scientists study the movement and formation of the pack ice in order to gather clues about wind patterns and climate.

The deep layer of ice which covers the **plateau** in the vast interior of Antarctica reveals vital information about the world's climatic trends. Its crystals contain the trapped air of many thousands of years, and if scientists can get at this air and analyse it they are accessing ancient environmental records. It is like listening to Stone Age weather forecasts. This obviously involves getting the ice out—not an easy task if it's a mile deep.

The main work involved in this branch of Antarctic science is the recovery of **ice cores** by drilling. The further down you go, the older the ice, so it is the deep stuff that yields the most valuable data. Ice from a deep core is packed with compressed air bubbles—if you hack it up on a chopping board it fizzes like Alka-Seltzer. Once the cores are out, they have to be transported home on a refrigerated ship—and the person who turns off the electricity by mistake is in big trouble. When the cores reach the home institution, they are stored in freezers like white logs in a meat-packing warehouse. At Vostok, the Russian station in East Antarctica, scientists have drilled deeper than anyone else, so they have the world's oldest ice. An analysis of ice cores reveals changes to atmospheric gases such as carbon dioxide over the past 10,000 years.

The dynamics and mass balance of the ice sheet and glaciers and the relationship of Antarctic ice to regional and global weather and ocean processes is also studied by **ice surveys** from land and air. In 1993–5, for example, an Australian team undertook an ambitious overland circuit of the Lambert Glacier. Scientists are interested in the response of the ice cap to climate change and the consequent impacts on sea levels.

The West Antarctic **ice streams** are very important to scientists working in the field of ice mechanics and glacial processes. The aim of investigating ice-stream dynamics is to establish whether the Antarctic ice sheet is stable. There are half a dozen ice streams on the West Antarctic ice sheet: they are fast-flowing currents of ice *embedded within the ice sheet*, and they are up to 50 miles wide and 310 miles long (80km by 500km). They are cited as evidence of possible glacial retreat and the much-touted imminent rise in global sea levels. Ice streams are not well understood. To start with, they are remote, so even more difficult for scientists to get to than most Antarctic field sites. When they do get there, they drill boreholes to the bottom of the ice streams and lower in instruments which gather data until they are recovered the following year. The data yielded has revealed that the base of at least some of the streams is at melting point. So the streams are moving—they are not frozen into position. These motions provide a process for rapid dispersal and disintegration of this vast quantity of ice. This means that most of the drainage of this unstable western ice sheet occurs through the ice streams. By studying them, scientists learn about the interactive role of the ice sheet in global change.

So it seems that *if* the ice melted, resulting in the fabled Great Flood of the popular press, water would pour out of the continent, via the ice streams, on the Siple Coast, virtually the only part of Antarctica not bounded by mountains.

Geology

As we have seen, about 0.4 per cent of Antarctic consists of exposed rock; the rest is concealed under an ice blanket. But the fact that we can't see it doesn't mean it isn't there: Antarctica is a continent with mountains and valleys and a vastly variegated topography like any other. It is, on average, three times higher than any other continent.

Scientists are keen to draw a map of this land—they want to find out what the earth is like underneath its white cover. It's a tricky business. Because of the inconvenient ice cover, most Antarctic geology can only be studied by remote-sensing methods like **seismology**. This involves using explosives to find out what the ground is like under 6000 feet of ice. The explosions bounce soundwaves down through the ice to the earth's crust, and scientists record the waves on their way back up. The explosives, usually orange sausages of nitroglycerine and a fibrous absorption material, have to be buried in a series of 90ft holes in the ice, and the most difficult part of the work is making the holes. Each one is begun using a self-contained unit which heats water and sprinkles it on the ice like a shower head.

Seismology is a tool, and in Antarctica it operates either by **refraction** or **reflection**, the difference between the two being largely a function of scale in that reflection facilitates the imaging of a smaller area in greater detail. In the case of refraction, soundwaves from the explosions are refracted back to the surface from the earth's sediment and recorded by a line of Ref Teks, the soundwave equivalent of the tape recorder. The Ref Teks contain computers hooked up to geophones, and as many as 90 Ref Teks are placed 200 yards apart on a line. They remain in place for the whole science season, and data is downloaded to larger computers and returned to the home institution for analysis.

A lot of geological research is concerned with an understanding of earlier **supercontinents**. Lesser (or West) Antarctica is a hypothesised rift system—a jumble of unstable plates—separated from the stable shield of Greater (or East) Antarctica by the Transantarctics. On top, most of Lesser Antarctica consists of the world's only marine-based ice sheet. This means that the bottom of the ice is far below sea level, and if it all melted, a large portion of Antarctica would consist of a group of islands. The assemblage of plates which make up Lesser Antarctica have been moving both relative to one another and to the east for something like 230 million years, whereas Greater Antarctica, home of the polar plateau, has existed relatively intact for many hundreds of millions of years. In Gondwana, the prehistoric supercontinent, what we now know as South America and the Antipodes were joined to Antarctica. Gondwana started to break up early in the Jurassic Period—say 175 million years ago—and geologists like to speculate on the relationship of Antarctica to still earlier supercontinents.

Fossils are an intrinsic part of this branch of Antarctic science. Rocks near Australia's Davis Station, for example, have been found to hold fossils that are four million years old. Several whale skeletons have been discovered there (all extinct forms). They are the only

Antarctic vertebrate fossils formed since the development of the circumpolar current. Antarctica once had no ice at all—it was like a tropical rain forest. It even had its own **dinosaurs**. They roamed around among trees such as a deciduous beech almost identical to an indigenous species prolific in today's Tasmania.

Medical Research

As Antarctica is such an extreme environment it is a useful laboratory to assess human behaviour and physiology (*see also* **Living in Antarctica**, p.83). What is the effect of total natural light deprivation, for example? Do men and women adapt differently to the cold? What immunological changes take place in such a germ-free environment? Other projects have included studies of energy levels, sleep patterns, blood lipid levels, flexibility of joints, dehydration, circulatory changes, the growth rate of hair and nails, and thermal stress in divers. Australian doctors have discovered that lengthy stays in Antarctica results in reduced skin immune responses. Their research is continuing with studies on the interaction of the brain and endocrine glands with the immune system, looking specifically at lymphocyte function, virus reactivation and hormone concentrations.

Antarctic programmes often collaborate with other research bodies on projects with direct application to human experiences off the ice. Studies of the natural daily body rhythm and its association with the daylight cycle have provided an insight both into jet lag and sleeping problems with shift workers. Both NASA and the European Space Agency have used the winter isolation of Antarctic bases to look at how microbes are passed between people. Physiological investigations of scientific divers in the Antarctic have been extended to divers operating in other cold-water areas, for example police forensic diving teams.

HYDROPONICS ON BASE

Living in Antarctica

Although Antarctica has no indigenous population, several thousand scientists and support staff make it their home each summer and about a thousand live through the long months of winter darkness. It takes a good deal of effort to sustain safe, healthy and comfortable living conditions on the ice.

Clothing

Technology has produced a welter of new fabrics which insulate the human body against cold and wind while facilitating freedom of movement and the evaporation of sweat. Most of the clothes worn in Antarctica are specially developed for polar conditions and are not available on the high street. They are bought or commissioned by the various Antarctic programmes and lent to participants.

Each national programme has a clothing department or section which keeps up with developments in fibre technology. Everyone who has visited McMurdo or South Pole with the US programme is familiar with the procedure at the USAP offices in Christchurch, New Zealand, which is the point of departure for these two Antarctic stations. Having sent in your measurements ahead of time, you are given an appointment at the clothing store and turn up to find a mound of gear waiting with your name on. You then try on all these items and exchange any which don't fit until you have a whole Antarctic wardrobe. And this is quite an impressive quantity of gear.

Everything works on the layer principle. Trapped air acts as insulation, and layers can be taken on and off as conditions fluctuate or you begin to sweat. (If sweat does not evaporate, the moisture freezes, which means clothes are cold and heavy. This is what happened to the cosy furs worn by early explorers. Also, furs are very heavy even before they freeze, which means precious extra calories are burned wearing them—a grave disadvantage to the sledger.) Typically, you start off with long johns and a long-sleeved thermal vest. In colder than average conditions you would probably wear an expedition-weight (i.e. heavier) set of underwear on top of the first. Then you put on heavy-duty windpants, for example, or special fabric salopettes or dungarees, or moleskin or fibre-pile trousers, and a long-sleeved heavy woollen shirt and polarfleece jacket. The parka, or anorak, is the most important item. It is usually stuffed with down and has a fur-trimmed hood. The pockets are so numerous that small items, once deposited within them, may never be seen again.

The British Antarctic Survey is well known for its loyalty to old-fashioned design reminiscent of Captain Scott. BAS employees still wear enormous over-the-head smock-style windproofs (now made of cotton ventile) and matching trousers of the kind sported by Scott and his party in the famous photograph of the five of them looking dejected at the South Pole after they realised Amundsen had beaten them to it (*see* after p.138).

Gloves are of critical importance, as the extremities are the first to succumb to frostbite. A pair of polypropylene gloveliners are worn underneath more substantial gloves, the latter perhaps made of leather, or fibre-pile mittens. In very cold conditions bearpaws are worn—huge great fur-lined canvas or waxed cotton affairs.

At home you'd usually take off your gloves for jobs such as refuelling a vehicle or checking the oil. In Antarctica you could easily get frostbite while engaged in such a simple activity, especially if it's windy. Men and women working with vehicles usually keep a separate pair of fuel gloves for such purposes to avoid smelling of petrol.

A good deal of heat is lost through the head, so hats are very important. They are usually made of some kind of thermal fabric, with or without a fur trim. If the wind is blowing it is advisable, and often essential, to ensure that no flesh is in direct contact with the wind, and a balaclava is worn for this purpose. People tuck it under goggles to ensure that not a single inch of flesh is exposed. In the winter a neoprene face mask may be added to the ensemble. The neck is prone to heat loss on account of the fat jugular vein which lies near the surface, and polypropylene neck gaiters, slipped on over the head, deal with the problem. Snow goggles or glacier glasses are essential to protect the eyes against snow-blindness, the result of the surface of the eye being burnt by ultraviolet light: even on overcast days ultraviolet rays are reflected off the snow or ice, and snow-blindness is a crippling injury.

Footwear is a major issue and people on the ice spend a lot of time talking about it. Some kinds of boot require bootee-type fleecy liners, and some are insulated by air which means you have to switch a valve on and off when in a pressurised plane. Some programmes—for example the British Antarctic Survey—issue rubber-bottomed, leather-upper boots. Interchangeable felt insoles are useful. One school of thought is that only one pair of socks should be worn, in order to maximise heat conservation and sweat evaporation, but many people wear more.

Accommodation

Bases these days are very comfortable, boasting electricity and running water. Most bases even have beds, or at least bunks, and at McMurdo some of the rooms have television sets and telephones. Some bases now have two-person bedrooms, but most require four or six people to share. New materials are always being weather-tested and bases are becoming more comfortable and more secure against the depredations of weather. A variety of building materials have been deployed: the Australians have been very successful, for example, with steel frames on concrete foundations with an external skin of six-inch-thick panels of steel-clad polystyrene foam. Fire is always a hazard in the dry Antarctic climate. Emergency stores of food, communications equipment and survival gear are stored away from the main station building as a precaution against fire.

Personnel are expected to contribute to the running of the station; broadly speaking, the smaller the station, the more burdensome the duties. At a medium-sized base with a summer population of between thirty and forty there is usually a full-time cook, while other housekeeping duties are shared between everyone else on a rota system. Each base has its own system and its own colloquialisms for housekeeping duties—the British use the word 'gash', the Australians 'slushy' and the Americans 'haus maus'. One person is normally assigned the job of nightwatch in order to protect the base against fire. This role is generally carried out on a weekly rota basis, and other duties, such as nightly weather observations, turning on the bread ovens and waking people up in the morning, are included. People tend to look forward to their turn on nightwatch as it affords a spell of solitude—a rare commodity in Antarctica, where one is never completely alone.

On a small station scientists have to act as their own cook, diesel mechanic and radio operator, but on larger bases these jobs are all done by a specialist.

Over half the forty Antarctic stations that operate all year round are clustered in the region of the Antarctic Peninsula, the wonky finger which extends from the continent towards South America. McMurdo Station, on the opposite side, is the home of Antarctica's largest human community. Established on Ross Island in 1956, it has grown from an outpost of a few shacks to a small town of more than 100 buildings and, in summer, as many as 1300 people. The winter population is about 250. McMurdo has saunas, two bars and a coffee shop, a gymnasium, a basketball court and a bowling alley.

South Pole Station, also owned by the Americans, is largely sheltered under an aluminium geodesic dome 165ft in diameter at the base and about 50ft high at the apex. The dome houses two-storey structures containing living, communications and laboratory facilities. A series of steel arches runs perpendicular to the axis of the dome's main entryway and houses the garage complex, gymnasium, carpenter shop, power plant, biomedical facility (known to insiders as Club Med) and main fuel storage. During the winter all personnel (there are normally about 27 of them) live under the dome. In the summer visiting scientists and some support staff live in outlying huts in an area known to residents as summer camp. This is also the emergency facility for the winter crew.

Portrait of a Base

Terra Nova Bay is a medium-sized permanent base on the coast of the Antarctic continent at latitude 74°S and longitude 164°E. Terra Nova was established by the Italians after the site was identified by their first expedition, which took place during the 1985–6 season. It lies on the fringe of the Northern Foothills and is dominated by Mount Melbourne.

TNB remains the sole Italian station in Antarctica, and it is occupied only during the summer months. Access is by Italian air force Hercules, flown by a Pisa-based squadron, via Christchurch, New Zealand. A runway has been cleared on the sea ice of Terra Nova Bay, but this becomes unusable when the ice starts to melt around the beginning of December, and at that point the Italians are dependent on their supply ship.

Seawater is desalinated by reverse osmosis, and treated waste water is discharged into a small cove. The base buildings cover about 40,000 square feet, and this includes accommodation for 60 people and a wide range of science facilities.

Outside two double-wall tanks store fuel. Electricity is supplied by four generators. Vehicles include cranes, loaders, tractors, skidoos, a research boat and four dinghies with outboard motors.

The Italian programme conducts a wide range of scientific research, including the study of background electromagnetic radiation. A new observatory has been built, and results are measured in submillimetre and infrared wavelengths. As far as other Antarcticans are concerned, however, it is the quality of the cuisine that distinguishes Terra Nova Bay. Many scientific theories have been postulated requiring a field trip to take measurements at the Italian base...

Camping

In the field, most people live in **tents**. These are often two-person pyramid tents specially designed to withstand high winds and wind-driven ice particles. Americans call them Scott tents and the British call them pyramid tents. Although the two types look the same at first glance, the entrance to a pyramid is two feet off the ground, making entry and exit harder and reflecting the higher levels of snow accumulation on the Antarctic Peninsula—the 'British' sector of the continent. The Scott tents used by Americans are less steeply angled.

Many different kinds of transportable **huts** are in use for field-work. Many are taken from base in pieces and assembled on site. These include **weatherhavens**, arched tents 12ft long and 6ft wide with board flooring. A permanently lit tilley lamp is usually hanging from the ceiling of a weatherhaven as there is no other form of heating. Similarly, the standard interior decor is an array of dripping gloves and hats dangling from an overhead network of string.

Jamesways are ubiquitous in long-term American field camps and constitute the heart of camp, too, like the kitchen in a farmhouse. An invention of the military, Jamesways are portable, insulated tents of standard width and height but variable length—to make them longer, you add more arches. They have board floors and a proper door, and in Antarctica are heated by drip-oil Preways. The latter are massive heaters fed by a barrel strapped to the outside of the hut. Jamesways are often left up during the winter and occupied for many consecutive summers by scientists returning to collect data.

Some camps consist of a number of Jamesways and several science projects working at the same location—there might be as many as fifty people on one site. In such cases, a full-time cook or two is generally employed by the programme as well as several field assistants. Smaller camps are much more common, however: in some cases a field camp consists of two men and a tent. Many camps are large enough to have an electricity generator, which are required for certain kinds of scientific equipment—but many people feel that they blight the perfect Antarctic silence.

Between a hut and a tent, fibreglass igloos known as **Apples** are also used in small science camps, and, like several other kinds of Antarctic hut, they can be towed to the site by a large vehicle such as a sno-cat or slung under a helicopter and swung along. Extended apples are known as **Melons**, and elongated apples inevitably as **Zucchinis**.

Whether living in a hut or a tent, in the field the rugged Antarctican sleeps in a sleeping bag. In the olden days men had reindeer hair bags. They smelt of sour bread after a good soaking, and weighed a ton, which meant they weren't exactly suitable for sledging. Nowadays they come in various models, according to temperature requirements, and a tour of the store at the Berg Field Center at McMurdo Station reveals stacks of neatly labelled bags ending with 'Snowy Owl. Minus Fifty Degrees'. Often double bags are used if it's very cold. These consist of a down-filled outer bag and a synthetic pile-filled inner version. Some bags have mummy-style hoods, and they are all very narrow at the feet, unlike old-fashioned camping bags at home, as this shape minimises the amount of air the hapless camper has to warm before he or she has any chance of slumber. The British camper also goes into the field equipped with an inflatable airbed and a sheepskin under-blanket, but other nationalities consider this feeble.

Food and Drink

It's a well-known fact that people eat more when they are cold. The body needs calories to produce its own heat, and of course, food is a great psychological comforter too. Hard work in a cold climate requires a huge amount of calories—pulling a sledge all day over sastrugi, for example (wind-whipped snow-waves) can burn up as many as 8000 calories. It's very hard to pack this much food if you are trying to keep weight down, which is why explorers tend to eat energy-intensive foods such as butter.

Until the 1950s everybody ate pemmican, a particularly revolting dried beef meat and fat mixture developed by the Hudson Bay Company from Eskimo origins. In the early days of Antarctic exploration men often contracted scurvy, a painful and potentially fatal condition caused by a lack of vitamin C. Scott's second-in-command, Teddy (later Admiral Sir Teddy) Evans almost died of it. Too much of certain vitamins can also be dangerous: a few years after Scott perished Douglas Mawson suffered vitamin A poisoning in Antarctica as a result of eating husky livers.

Neither condition is prevalent in Antarctica nowadays. Everybody eats well, even in the field—there just isn't much fresh food. The winter is a particularly challenging period for the Antarctic cook as there are no supplies during the long months of darkness. Complex carbohydrates are a staple in the form of packet rice and pasta. Tins of vegetables, fruit and sauces are widely used, as are dehydrated veg and packet sauces. Mashed potato out of a packet, dehydrated cottage cheese, freeze-dried strawberries and lots of chocolate—all this features on the Antarctic menu. Packet soups are popular (and often constitute a techno-logical achievement as they are completely tasteless) as is dried fruit. BAS still issues ration boxes for use in the field, and about 3500 calories per day are allowed. This is made up of about 3.5 ounces of protein, 7 ounces of fat and six ounces of carbohydrate. Primus-type stoves are used in the field, and in the case of more established camps, gas ovens are also available. Some old BAS huts even have enormous Agas.

Cooking up delicious meals in the field constitutes something of a challenge, but people rise to the occasion, often taking it in turns to see who can produce the most appetizing spread. Resupply helicopters or planes often bring a small bag of fresh goods and these are eagerly awaited. Nobody wants trouble these days and so most bases are ridiculously over-stocked with food. As a result, everything is years past its sell-by date in Antarctica. This never seems to have adverse effects on the hungry consumers, though many things disintegrate when they come into contact with water as they have passed through so many temperature changes.

Water

On coastal bases, reverse osmosis plants often are installed to turn seawater into fresh. Other kinds of desalination plants are in use. The salt water distillation plant at McMurdo distils seawater at a rate of about 50,000 gallons per day; on inland bases, glacier ice or chunks of ice-sheet have to be melted.

As a result, water is quite precious. In summer, melt streams are occasionally used in the field, but generally campers take it in turns to collect 'glacier berries'—chunks of ice which have fallen off the nearest glacier—or to pickaxe ice bricks off a glacier cliff. A giant ice-cube will then be set on a pot on top of a stove.

As Antarctica is one of the driest places on earth it is very important to drink far more than usual. An insulated water-bottle is a very useful piece of kit and some people make rules for themselves, for example drinking a pint or two of water before breakfast. Packets of high-energy powdered fruit drinks are popular, and some people find this helps them ingest their required dose of fluid. Milk comes in various forms—powder, tins and tubes—though none of it bears much resemblance to what once emerged from the cow.

Reverse Osmosis: or How to Drink Seawater

Osmosis is the movement of a fluid or solution through a membrane (which is basically a filter with microscopic holes). The membrane generally separates two solutions of different ionic concentrations. The fluids can pass through the membrane, but if the ions are too big they cannot. Commonly, one of the two fluids is water, and that 'moves into' the other solution, ultimately to change that solution's ion concentrations.

In reverse osmosis, water is forced in the other direction by a pressure gradient. In the case of reverse osmosis plants on Antarctic bases, seawater is stored on one side of a membrane and pressure is applied to it by a pump. Fluid is therefore forced through the membrane. That membrane acts as a filter to take salt from the seawater, leaving pure water as the fluid on the other side of the membrane.

The process of forcing fluid through microscopic holes is a difficult thing to do rapidly, and the technology to make it happen on a large scale is quite expensive. The many people who live on well systems in the USA usually have small reverse osmosis units in the house to treat groundwater. Typically, a family would have a five-gallon tank under the sink to purify their water.

Over Snow and Ice

'Dogs like that, which share man's hard times and strenuous work, cannot be looked upon merely as animals. They are supporters and friends. There is no such thing as making a pet out of a sledge dog; these animals are worth much more than that.'

Helmer Hanssen, Amundsen's dog-handler

In the old days, sledges were pulled by dog-teams. In 1991 the Antarctic Treaty nations declared that under the terms of the Environmental Protocol to the Treaty huskies were to be 'phased out' of Antarctica by 1 April 1994. The British were still breeding dogs at that time, but when this announcement was made the programme was stopped immediately. BAS had kept dogs continually since 1945, though they hadn't been essential to scientific work for several years. With the advent of reliable snowmobile travel, the dogs had become increasingly obsolete and had been retained primarily for recreational purposes. Besides mechanization, another argument for the removal of the dogs was the suggestion that they passed on canine distemper to seals, and, more plausibly, that the seal chop necessitated by their voracious appetites was 'inappropriate to the environmental aims of scientific organisations within the Antarctic.'

Today there are many solutions to the problem of how to transport people and equipment in Antarctica. The one constant, of course, is skiing. Cross-country skis are used at all stations during the summer, and at places where the winter weather is slightly less harsh they are used in the dark months too.

Skidoos are also widely used. Also called snowmobiles, most skidoos have a two-stroke engine and can tow loads well in excess of a thousand pounds. They resemble large motor-bikes on caterpillar tracks with a front ski, and the low ground pressure of this system protects machine and rider against cracks in sea ice or soft snow. People are always being told to wear crash helmets while riding, but in practice hardly anyone does. **Sledges** are hitched to the back of skidoos and towed. The most popular kind of sledge remains the **Nansen**, designed by Fridtjof Nansen for Arctic travel in the 1890s. Nails and screws are not used in the construction of a Nansen sledge. The wooden parts are lashed together with twine and raw-hide thongs, thereby allowing flexibility as the sledge is pulled over hillocky ice. Skidoos are very popular in the south, especially with the boys, who like to race them. The theory is that you should ride standing up, with one knee on the seat, in order to be able to leap off quickly in the event of a major bump. It seems more likely that an excess of testosterone prevents anything as un-macho as sitting down to ride.

For heavy-duty work around station, **sno-cats** or caterpillar trucks are used. A popular make is the American Tucker; other makes, such as the Canadian Bombadier Muskegs, have hydraulic cranes on the rear and no cabs. Again, rubber-belted tracks mean low ground pressure. As many as eight people can be transported in the heated cab. Among the largest sno-cats ever used are the legendary **D-8** low ground pressure tractors with 54-inch treads. The diesel engine is started by a gasoline engine, making the machines particularly suitable for low temperatures. There are only about six stretch D-8s still is use in the world, and three live at Williams (Willy) Field, an outpost of McMurdo station about a mile from the main buildings. The enormous canary yellow machines were made by Caterpillar in the Fifties and have seen 40 years' Antarctic service. They have walked themselves to the Pole, and they have flown there dismantled (this takes four flights). One of them, at Byrd Surface Camp on the West Antarctic ice sheet, is back in use after spending 17 years buried under the snow. The catwalk platforms once fixed above the tread have regrettably been removed: veterans can remember seeing operators sunbathing on the platforms while the machine was moving along.

One of the main functions of a D-8 is bulldozing snow. A vast blade is fitted for this purpose; other tractors with a 'dozing capacity have a smaller blade. BAS use a British-built machine, the International Harvester. It weighs over eight tons and is fitted with extended and widened tracks to enable it to work in snow.

Large rubber-tracked all-terrain vehicles, for example Hägglunds (of Swedish military provenance) and Sprytes are also common. A Hägglunds has two watertight fibreglass cabs which allegedly enable it to float.

By Air

Four-engine **Hercules** planes are used by several Antarctic programmes. Most of these are LC-130s, and they can land on ski or on wheels, but on ski their cargo capacity is much reduced. Landing strips are cleared on sea ice (as at Terra Nova Bay), or on the permanent ice of an ice shelf (as at Williams Field near McMurdo), or simply on the polar plateau (as at the South Pole). Twin-engine planes are also in use, notably de Havilland **Twin Otters**, which can also land on ski or wheels. Gravel airstrips have been built for these planes in several places, for example at the Chilean Base Marsh on King George Island. The normal range of a Twin Otter is about 500 miles with a 2000lb load, but they can travel further if equipped with extra fuel tanks. British Otters make a trip in excess of 1000 miles, for example, from Rothera Station on Adelaide Island across the Antarctic Peninsula and the Brunt Ice Shelf to Halley Station. Otters normally fly between 5000 and 10,000ft, but they can go up to 21,000ft. Recently British pilots have begun landing a four-engine **Dash-7** plane on blue ice (plateau ice ablated of snow) which means scientists and gear can be transported to remote field sites more cheaply and in a less labour-intensive way (they have hitherto been ferried by Twin Otter). All planes return to the real world for overhaul in the winter.

Helicopters are invaluable for scientific work as they can get people to otherwise inaccessible spots—up in the Dry Valleys, for example, or to mountainous areas on the fringes of the continent where crypto-endolithic microbes lurk under the surfaces of sandstone scoured of snow. Until recently, the airborne squadron of the US Navy, VXE-6, undertook all helicopter flying for the US programme. The work is now carried out by a private firm. The Australians use Sikorsky S-76 helos which can carry people up to 215 miles.

On Water

Most Antarctic programmes own or commission **ships**. Since 1954, for example, all Australia's Antarctic stations have been served by ice-strengthened ships. Vessels can only reach Antarctica during the summer months, as in the winter the coastal sea is frozen. For voyages early in the season, in some cases ships drop anchor up against the edge of the frozen ice off the coast, up to 50 miles from the station. Cargo and personnel are then transported by helicopter or, if the sea ice is thick enough, by tracked vehicle.

Many of the ships are **icebreakers**, for example the Australian RSV *Aurora Australis*, which can break ice four feet thick at a steady 2.5 knots. Most icebreakers used by polar programmes are also research vessels, equipped with laboratories.

Coastal stations keep a number of inflatable boats with small outboard motors.

Communications

The seven territorial claimants issue special Antarctic stamps and operate a post office. They seem to think this reinforces their claim, but in fact all it does is provide material for philatelists (and thus a source of revenue). At all stations mail arrives during the summer, infrequently by ship and as often as once a week by plane, depending on the location. In winter there is no mail. Life on station has been transformed all year round by the advent of electronic mail, as it means that as long as they are sitting in front of a screen connected by satellite to the Internet expeditioners can talk to folk at home free of charge. A handful of field camps are now also on-line, and at some which are not, scientists send email back to base on disk, relying on base personnel to transmit it to its destination. The large stations have telephone links to the outside world.

The most important method of communication, however, is the radio, as this is how field camps check in once a day with base and pilots keep in touch with the station operations centre. High-frequency sets are used except when a very high frequency line-of-sight system is adequate. Setting up an aerial (antenna) is the first job in the queue upon arrival at a campsite, before even erecting the tent. Then a fixed time is arranged for the daily check-in. If the field party misses its check-in, a search-and-rescue mission will be mounted from base. Often the daily check-in constitutes a high point of the day, as campers enjoy contact with the outside world and often ask for news from base. Radio operators learn to be chatty and provide more than a simple communications check. They fulfil a psychological role too, and a relationship established over the airwaves can be of crucial importance later should an emergency situation develop.

Given the importance of the radio and its critical role as an emergency aid in a survival situation, the issue of keeping batteries alive in viciously low temperatures in one that has exercised many Antarctic minds. Rule number one is always to keep a spare battery for your hand-held VHF radio stowed within the inner folds of your garments so it remains warm. Rule two is to recharge all your batteries when you are on station or in a camp large enough to have its own generator. Rule three is always, always have spare and fully charged HF radio batteries in camp. Believe it or not, solar power is popular in Antarctica—the ambient temperature may be low, but the sun does shine for 24 hours a day for half the year, and the energy released can recharge batteries and power lights.

Leisure

Although maintaining a camp and even a station consumes a good deal of energy, there are many leisure hours, especially in the winter and when white-out conditions in summer mean no field science can be undertaken. Camp life revolves around science, nonetheless, and when a storm closes in it revolves around conversations about the weather. In a tent there is little scope for leisure pursuits beyond reading, playing cards and, when things get really desperate, going through the alphabet naming ten cities beginning with each letter, then ten rivers, and so on. On their 1992–3 attempted traverse of the continent Mike Stroud and Ran Fiennes relaxed at night by playing chess using urine sample bottles.

On base there are far more opportunities for creative leisure. Besides the usual pursuits (drinking, hanging out, reading, board games, sketching and so on) people have even been known to put on plays and organise art shows (there is an annual art show on Ross Island). At McMurdo a knitting group, informally known as Stitch'n'Bitch, meets once a week. Photography is a major hobby, especially during the winter when expeditioners hide away in dark room developing their summer films. Over these months of polar night all sorts of evening-school classes are held, from languages to iron-welding. Watching videos is popular, but can get wearing if there isn't an adequate supply. Those who spend the whole winter on base have been known to be able to recite certain screenplays by heart. British stations have a weekly communal video-viewing system and people take it in turns to choose a film. Sometimes a particularly malicious individual selects a terrible film and then walks out after five minutes, leaving his colleagues to stew over it.

Various events punctuate the year, for example the midwinter polar plunge at Scott Base when people strip naked and plunge into McMurdo Sound through a specially made hole in the ice. Several programmes have regular running races and award certificates to participants, and until recently an annual golf tournament was held at Williams Field, called the Ice Pines (balls were painted fluorescent colours). On the peninsula the British men at Rothera gamely battle on in the hangar during the winter (when the planes are back in England) playing badminton—always a struggle, as the shuttlecocks shatter in the cold. Radio darts tournaments are also popular and afford massive scope for cheating. Midwinter Dinners have been staged on 21 June since before Captain Scott's day to mark the half-way point of the long Antarctic night, and the tradition lives on. British Antarcticans each make a midwinter gift for one other man on station, and these are ceremoniously exchanged after a bibulous banquet. Whilst some of the gifts look like the work of a three-year-old, many men spend months in the carpentry shop or hunched over a canvas and produce truly fabulous gifts which are treasured forever.

Some leisure events reflect the cultural proclivities of the host nation. Who else but the Americans would host a Chilli Cook-Off, inviting participants to produce vats of chilli *con* or *sin carne* (preferably while wearing fancy dress). A panel of judges march round a number of open-air stalls in the centre of McMurdo, tasting each dish, and a spokesperson eventually announces a winner.

The Chileans operate a radio station which broadcasts to all bases on King George Island, and the schedule includes a Friday-night quiz show. All the questions are about Antarctica and the winner is obliged to come to Marsh, the Chilean station, to collect the prize. The only trouble is, you have to speak Spanish to join in. This is no problem for the Uruguayans and the Argentinians, who also have bases on King George Island, and the Brazilians can just about cope, but the Russians and the Poles struggle and the Chinese lag very far behind indeed.

The large, mixed stations, of which there are few, obviously present other opportunities for recreation, and a couple of seasons ago a female worker left McMurdo on the first flight after the station opened at the end of winter because she was pregnant.

Medical Facilities

Of course, the problem with getting sick in Antarctica is that you probably can't get to a hospital. In winter this is certainly the case, and even in summer the chances of swift evacuation are small. As a result, medical facilities on station are very sophisticated. All the larger bases have doctors specially trained in cold-weather medicine. They are normally engaged on a twelve-month tour. In addition, several people on each base are trained as nursing and anaesthetic assistants. Every field camp is equipped with medical kits, and everyone who goes south receives some kind of basic first-aid training with particular reference paid to cold-weather injury such as frostbite and hypothermia. There are no dentists (although sometimes one visits on a ship) so doctors are sent on a dental course prior to deployment. Antarctic doctors are always keen to practise their newly acquired dental skills. Beware!

Antarctica is a challenge to the base doctor as he or she must be a specialist in all areas. And of course if the doctors get sick, they must treat themselves. Everyone in the south is familiar with the story of the Soviet doctor who, in 1961, was obliged to remove his own appendix. Some people have chosen to have elective appendectomies before going south, but medical opinion is mostly against this.

Contrary to what you might expect, colds and flu are rare on the ice. There are few bacteria, and, especially during the winter, no influxes of new germs. Usually the winter crew all go down with a cold when a ship or Hercules brings the first lot of summer personnel. During the summer some people find perpetual daylight desynchronizing and experience difficulty sleeping. This is known as the 'Big Eye' phenomenon.

As you might expect in such a challenging environment, base staff are always willing to treat other nationals if they have superior facilities. This often occurs when stations are near enough to transport patients and one has a mobile operating theatre. On one occasion a Russian helicopter flew an injured Australian who was bleeding from a ruptured ulcer from Davis (Australian) to Mirny (Russian). From there he was transferred to a ski-equipped Hercules which flew to McMurdo (American) and from there on to New Zealand for surgery.

The doctors are usually, and hopefully, the most under-employed people on base, so they often conduct research studies on the physiological and psychological effects of Antarctica upon the human organism. These sometimes involve taking blood, which temporarily makes doctors the most unpopular characters on station. The doctors must also learn to be innovative. One Australian scientist lost both glasses and contact lenses during the course of a season, so the doctor organised new spectacle lenses to be ground out of perspex in the station workshop according to a prescription read out over the radio by an ophthalmologist in Australia. Dentures have been repaired with teeth fashioned from those of a seal, though it is true that this hasn't happened recently. Telemedicine—diagnosis by satellite—has been used successfully for many years: digitised images of X-rays, for example, can be sent home for expert opinion.

The body is well taken care of all over Antarctica but only the larger bases have the capacity to nourish the soul. The Chileans (at Marsh) and the Americans (at McMurdo) have established chapels, the former Catholic and the latter multidenominational.

Other Safety Issues

Everyone who goes to Antarctica is required to undergo survival training. This takes place at home before departure, for example ocean survival skills courses in swimming pools, abseiling lessons in the mountains of the home nation and weekends away for lectures and practical lessons in all aspects of Antarctic life. Upon arrival on the ice the Americans send everyone to Survival School. Known as Happy Camp by veterans, over a few days participants learn how to build a snow shelter in the event of losing their tent or crashing in a helicopter. Many other skills are covered: how to saw ice blocks, how to rig up an HF antenna, how to light a primus when all the parts are freezing, how to revive a frostbitten extremity, how to detect hypothermia in a colleague—and the list continues. Back on base other courses are run to suit particular requirements—how to travel on sea ice, for example. (It is very important to learn how to drill sea ice to test its thickness, otherwise you will fall in.)

Everyone comes away from these courses much chastened. They learn just how dangerous living in Antarctica can be.

The Isolation Factor

Antarctica has earned itself the reputation as a place where people go barking mad. There they are, removed from everything they know and everyone they love, with no chance of escape. The story goes that a Soviet once killed a colleague on station with an ice-pick over an argument about a game of chess, and when the Americans first arrived on Ross Island they were obliged to line a hut with mattresses to create a padded cell for one of the Navy men. Many camps have no telephones, and most of those that do offer limited and expensive access. Sometimes a camp might consist of two people. Scientists for NASA and other space agencies have been using Antarctica for some time as a kind of human laboratory to assess the long-term effects of isolation in space.

Most scientists only spend a couple of months on the ice, but support staff regularly go for 12 or 18 months and the British send men for 2½ years, by which time they are ill-equipped to talk about anything except skidoos and how to light your own farts. Most of the mythology is based on isolated incidents, however, and psychologists who have studied the effects of the long months of darkness and confinement come up with conclusions which give one confidence in the ability of the human spirit to rise to any occasion. Of course people do get depressed in the winter when they are trapped on station. But only rarely does this depression develop into a medical condition or a chronic disorder.

Hygiene Issues

Toilet Facilities

This is of course by far the most fascinating topic, especially if you are English. On base toilets are generally of the porcelain variety, or at least the portable types with seats, lids, doors that close and so on. In the field, toilet arrangements vary according to the size and sophistication of the camp and the environmental requirements of the type of ice upon which it is located.

On sea ice it is generally permitted to deposit human waste through a hole in the ice. The difficulty arises when you try to drill through six feet of ice, and then even if you are successful you find, on a midnight visit to the facilities, that the hole has iced over. These problems can be overcome, however, and with a windbreaker around the loo and a wooden-box type lavatory with a styrofoam seat positioned over the hole, the sea-ice lav can be a very civilised model indeed—especially if you are careful enough to locate it with a stunning glacier view. Seals can cause problems if they shoot up through the hole and exhale. Pee-flags are acceptable at most camps. Their role is to limit the staining of the ice to one place.

A large camp on the plateau or the ice shelf warrants a special toilet hut with a door that closes and a system of bagging up the mercifully frozen contents (everyone's favourite job) and returning them to base for disposal. If such huts are not available or the camp is too small, you may be obliged to dig an underground chamber in order to escape the wind. People sometimes place empty fuel barrels in these chambers, with the lid prised off and a loo seat on top.

In some areas the need to preserve a pristine environment is so keenly felt that all human waste, liquid and solid, is flown out. The most notable of these areas is the region on the edge of the Antarctic continent opposite Ross Island, called the Dry Valleys, where scientists study nitrates in the soil and in the frozen lakes. In these valleys everyone is obliged to carry a pee-bottle with them, which are later emptied into barrels.

Many types of toilet have been introduced over the years, with varying degrees of success. Propane-fuelled varieties which burn solid waste once a day have been known to explode, and electric-powered loos are unpopular for the smell of cooking turds which they produce. Programmes with less environmental awareness simply allow their human waste to accumulate in a specifically designated dump site. Again, at least it is frozen.

The whole business is trickier for women than men. Pee-bottles are not women-friendly. Plastic funnels moulded into crotch-shape and fitted with a drainage tube are commercially available, and a small minority of women in the field use them. Most female Antarcticans find the effort involved in using these funnels disproportionate to the benefits, though the experience does become easier with practice. All Antarctic long johns, trousers and dungarees are fitted with a front slit as the manufacturers are apparently unaware that we no longer live in the Jurassic Age and there are indeed females of the species living and working on the ice. To use a pee-flag a woman is obliged to squat down in full view of everyone in camp and pull down however many pairs of legwear she has on. This does indeed happen, though it is something of an ordeal even for those of us who have spent far too many months of our lives in camps to worry about men seeing our bottoms. Often we succumb to the pressure and use a pee-bottle in the sanctuary of hut or tent, though this of course is contingent on the boys being absent from said hut, or it being physically possible to urinate into a narrow-necked bottle whilst lying horizontal in a one-person ridge tent.

Having Periods

A close second to going to the toilet in the league table of Most Gripping Topics Concerning Living in Antarctica. Until a couple of decades ago this was an issue most programmes could ignore as they maintained all-male bases and camps. It is still hardly a regularly aired topic, but a few ancient packs of sanitary towels are usually stashed away with the first-aid equipment and women arriving on the ice might be told in hurried tones that 'used sanitarywear' should not be put down any kind of toilet but placed in a special bin for blood products. The contents of these bins is flown out of Antarctica and incinerated somewhere else.

There is insufficient data to assess the affect of polar life upon the female menstrual cycle, which is a shame. A recent winter-over study at McMurdo station conducted by the doctor revealed that the cycles of the sixty-odd women on base that season synchronised very quickly.

Washing

Not a popular activity in the field. Low temperatures are a major disincentive when it comes to taking off your clothes. In fact it is probably true to say that most people camping in Antarctica never wash. A token strip wash takes place occasionally, but it is quite common to go for two months without washing one's hair, and in fact it is not particularly unhealthy, particularly in an environment where virtually nothing smells. In addition, collecting water takes a lot of effort—another demotivating factor. People hauling sledges across the continent on private expeditions do have to force themselves to wash every so often, or at least roll in the snow like a horse, in order to avoid painful sores from harnesses.

Wetwipes, also known as babywipes, are a boon in the field, as you can freshen up without taking any clothes off at all. They do freeze, however, so you need to make sure to keep them in a heated hut, or, if you do not have one, inside your sleeping bag. The only difficulty with this last solution is that once you have stowed your water bottle, batteries for tape recorders, laptops, Walkmen or science gear, plus some dry clothes for the morning in your bag, there may be little room for you in there.

Similarly, washing clothes is a pretty irregular business in the field (most bases, on the other hand, have washing machines). Various systems are deployed, such as turning underpants inside out, or waiting until a pair are so filthy that the dirty pair discarded last week come to seem clean.

Wildlife

With the exception of a handful of creatures barely visible to the naked eye, the Antarctic continent does not sustain non-migratory life. It is too harsh an environment. In the interior there is no water, and even in coastal regions it rarely rains and there is insufficient water to support terrestrial mammals. Indeed, the largest land animal in Antarctica is a winged midge about a quarter of an inch long. This is why penguins and seals have no fear—they have no land predators. (It also presents a stark contrast to the Arctic, where forty land mammals roam.) Even the marine mammals of Antarctica flee in the winter, with the exception of emperor penguins and Weddell seals who remain loyal to their Antarctic home during the long polar night. It's simply too cold and dark for anyone else.

Unlike the tropics, where species proliferate and thousands of sub-species evolve, polar regions are characterised by a paucity of species and an abundance of individuals. Around the coastal fringes, however, and on sub-Antarctic islands, a variety of specially adapted wildlife abounds during the explosive summer months of perpetual daylight. Life clings to the edge of Antarctica like iron filings to a magnet. Penguins and seals are the most familiar inhabitants, and there are also numerous species of seabird and several dozen mosses and lichens. The area has been referred to as the 'banana belt' by Antarctic veterans, since compared to the barren expanses of the polar plateau it seems positively tropical.

Unlike the continent itself, the Southern Ocean around it is teeming with a rich variety of life. It is up in the air and down under the water that wildlife proliferates in this desolate *terra incognita*.

Contrary to popular belief, there are no polar bears in the south. The reason penguins and polar bears never get into fights is quite simply that they never meet. Luckily for the penguins. There are no penguins in the Arctic: only the Galapagos penguin lives in the northern hemisphere.

Penguins are nature's satire on humanity, and they have become a symbol of Antarctica. Is any creature more widely loved, even by people—the majority—who will never see them, except in a zoo? They are ancient birds; fossils reveal that they were once 6ft tall. They were seen by white men for the first time at the end of the 15th century, and about 100 years later a Welshman named them 'white head' in his native tongue (*pen gwyn*).

There are seventeen species of penguin (though by no means all exist in the Antarctic), the most abundant variety breeding on the continent itself being the **Adélie** (*Pygoscelis adeliae*). There are as many as two and a half million breeding pairs of Adélies in the Antarctic. The scientific name *Pygoscelis*, which the Adélie shares with other species of penguin, means brushtailed, and the common name was bestowed by the French explorer Dumont d'Urville in honour of his wife. Adélies are smaller than kings and emperors, and classic in appearance, with no grey or orange markings. There heads are pure black, with eyes ringed with white, and they have stubby bills which are feathered to about an inch from the tip. They can live to be twenty. Adélies like to live on rocky, ice-free areas—there is a large colony at Cape Royds on Ross Island, for example, not far from Shackleton's hut. This is the most southerly colony in the world.

Like many creatures in the far south, Adélies (*right*) breed during the few balmy weeks of summer when the temperature rises above freezing. They spend the winter months further north, and the males are the first to return to the Antarctic breeding grounds after the arrival of the sun. Although they prefer to find the same mate as the previous year, the season is so short that if they are unable to find her they fairly quickly settle for someone else (this is one of their more human characteristics). Nests are made of pebbles and eggs are laid by mid-November and incubated for 30–40 days by both parents.

Hatching takes place in late December. All penguin chicks are fluffy when they are born, and most are lightish grey. Young Adélies look like puffballs, and after about ten days they moult and the first downy coat is replaced by a darker grey version. By mid-February the young have taken to the water. All penguins are extremely hydrodynamic. Adélies can swim at about 4½ miles an hour, and the maximum recorded

Adélie penguins nesting.

dive is 574ft. One of the most mesmerising sights of Antarctica is that of a trail of Adélies waddling to the edge of an ice floe and jumping in, feet first, descending in a line perpendicular to the water. When it is time to come out again, or a leopard seal is seen gliding through the depths, the penguins shoot out of the water as if they have been released by a tightly coiled spring. They land on their feet, always looking slightly surprised, as if they hadn't expected to land quite so soon. Like all penguins, they will drop down to their bellies and motor along the ice in a horizontal position if they reckon this is faster.

However long you spend in Antarctica, and however many thousands of these creatures you see, you will never stop anthropomorphising the penguin. Clergymen lining up at Synod, wine waiters attending table, a queue of shoppers at a bus stop—the analogies never run out. Despite the proliferation of Adélies on the continent itself, the best-known penguin is undoubtedly the **emperor** (*Aptenodytes forsteri*). Along with the Weddell seal and a few barely visible insects, the emperors (*below*) cheat the Antarctic winter. They breed in darkness, in the coldest conditions endured by any bird in the world. They arrive on fast ice in March or April, fattened up in preparation for the ordeal to come. After an elaborate and prolonged courtship ritual a single egg is laid in May or early June, and the male balances it on his scaly toes for 60-odd days of incubation, covered by a fold of abdominal skin. The birds huddle together during this dark time, rotating in order to take turns on the outside of the group, where they are flagellated by the wind. Females spend this period getting fat out at sea. Occasionally, the male abandons the egg before it has hatched, presumably as he is on the point of death by starvation, and makes a run for the ocean. When the chick emerges from the shell, mum comes back—although the chick takes its first feed from the emaciated male parent, who has lost almost half of his body weight during the winter. He feeds his baby with a secretion of fat and protein.

Emperor penguins on the ice.

The parents find each other in total darkness by cawing; each pair has its own special tune. Once the female is in place and the first feed has been given, the male goes off to sea to fatten up and females take over the nursery, regurgitating food to the infant (this is the normal penguin method of feeding). Soon the male returns again, his strength replenished, and the parents take it in turns to nurse as chicks learn to climb down from their mother's feet and stand on their own. Chicks fledge in the spring when they are about five months old, but the harsh conditions take their toll and many don't make it.

Emperors are sexually mature from about their fourth year. They breed in colonies all around the Antarctic coast and have been known to swim as far north as New Zealand, but this is rare. Adult birds weigh as much as 100lb and, with the neck extended, stand taller than 3ft. Their black heads have large yellow and white ear patches, and the upper breast is shaded with a pale yolky yellow. They are deep divers, and can go to almost 900 feet; they travel on the surface of the water they travel at about five miles an hour. Their diet is 95 per cent fish, 3 per cent squid and the rest crustaceans. Some live to be as old as 50.

After the emperor, the **king** (*Aptenodytes patagonica*) is the second largest penguin. Everyone knows what a king looks like as he appears on the chocolate-biscuit wrapper. He is perhaps the most handsome penguin: tall and slender, with a silvery grey back, distinctive mandarin-orange streaks around the ears and a sunset orange and yellow display on the top of the breast. A streak of orange characterises the lower half of the bill. The adult is over three feet tall and weighs about 26lb, which means it is slimmer than the emperor. Also, the orange markings are much darker and more vivid than those of the emperor, and more clearly delineated. It is this which gives the king the aesthetic edge. The male king goes in for sophisticated courtship displays, the object of which is to draw attention to his bright orange ear muffs. Like the emperors, kings are deep divers and have been known to go as far down as 800ft. Whereas the staple diet of the smaller penguins is krill, kings eat more squid and fish.

There are no king penguin colonies on the Antarctic continent. They breed on the islands, where the parents have access to the water throughout the winter to feed their chicks (emperors do not need to do this.) There is no nest, and a chick normally takes a year to fledge. Until they do, their thick brown down makes them look like teddy bears. Because of this long fledging period, kings do not breed annually, but once every two or three years.

The **gentoo** penguin (*Pygoscelis papua; right*) is another brush-tailed bird, featuring a red streak on the bill, a white patch on the brow and orange feet. It is

Gentoo penguin, South Georgia.

rather less aggressive than other Pygoscelis penguins (such as Adélies and chinstraps). On the continent itself gentoos only breed on the peninsula; most of them live in the tussock of sub-Antarctic islands, notably South Georgia. The further south they live, the smaller they are. They do not congregate in huge colonies but live in small numbers and are happy to cohabit with other species. Gentoos are the only penguins which continue to feed their young after fledging.

Of the three subspecies of **rockhopper** penguin, *Eudyptes chrysocome* lives the furthest south (though no further south than the tip of the peninsula). All rockhoppers are crested. They have spiky yellow head-feathers which protrude comically from behind the ear, joining a yellow stripe on the brow, bright red eyes and a long red bill. Their common name comes from the way they leap nimbly from rock to rock. The rockhopper is the smallest penguin in Antarctic regions, the adult measuring under two feet and weighing a little over five pounds.

The **macaroni** (*Eudyptes chrysolophus*) is another of the seven species of the crested penguin family. Macaronis do not live on the continent, but a large colony breeds on Elephant Island and there may be as many as five million pairs on South Georgia. 18th-century British sailors thought the floppy golden crests of these penguins resembled the plumed hats and frivolous hairdos of 'macaronis'—young London dandies named after Italian pasta. Macaronis are larger than rockhoppers, and have salmon bills and black heads.

The brush-tailed **chinstrap** (*Pygoscelis antarctica*) is another small penguin, its

BELOW (TOP TO BOTTOM):
• *Nesting rockhopper penguins, male and female.*
• *Macaroni penguin.*
• *Chinstrap penguin on the ice.*
OPPOSITE PAGE: A Weddell seal gives birth.

black cap seemingly held in place round its white neck by a thin black strap under its eye. Chinstraps are about 27 inches tall and most of the world's population live in the South Orkneys, the South Shetlands and the South Sandwich Islands.

Magellanic penguins (*Spheniscus magellanicus*) nest in colonies of up to a million birds and live in soil burrows like badgers. They have a thick white stripe around the eyes and ears, and bray like donkeys. This distinctive noise has earned them the alternative name jackass penguins. (There are other varieties of jackass, for example a South African version. All are of the Spheniscus variety, which means 'little wedge' and refers to the tail). Magellanic penguins were first encountered by Ferdinand Magellan when he circumnavigated the globe in the early 16th century. He took thousands of eggs and birds to provision his ships.

Seals

The seal's thick layer of blubber or fine fur acts as fine insulation. Although all seals have to come ashore to give birth, they can do so on sea ice and on the fast ice of an ice shelf, and are perfectly adapted to the Antarctic environment. Like penguins, they have no land predators in Antarctica.

The **fur seal** (*Arctocephalus gazella*) is the only eared seal in the Antarctic. The adult weighs up to 250lb (almost 18 stone) and is often longer than six feet. It is sleek, as its Latin name implies, with a thick neck and powerful chest, and its coarse coat is dark grey on top with a lighter belly. The ears are dainty. Preyed upon relentlessly during the 19th century, notably by American merchants taking skins to China, fur seals were persecuted to the verge of extinction. Numbers have recovered, and now the population is increasing each year. Fur seals live on the tip of the peninsula and on sub-Antarctic islands. They are especially fond of isolated rocks and islets.

All the other seals in the Southern Ocean are earless and insulated by blubber. The four main species are the Weddell, the leopard, the crabeater and the Ross. Of these, visitors are likely to have most experience of the **Weddell** (*Leptonychotes weddelli; giving birth, left*), which was named after the British whaling Captain James Weddell. Males can reach 11ft in

BELOW (TOP TO BOTTOM):
• *Weddell seal pup.*
• *Elephant seal, Falkland Islands.*
• *Crabeater seal on the ice.*

length and weigh 1000lb (71 stone!). The lovable Weddell is the most southerly mammal in the world, its coat owlish brown with a silvery spotty pattern. A large oxygen supply means the Weddell is an extremely efficient diver: during a deep dive its heartbeat slows to 75 per cent of its normal rate, and it can stay underwater for over an hour, as deep as 1300ft. Weddells are the only seals to spend the winter in the far south and they are able to do so as they have specially adapted teeth capable of keeping a breathing hole open in the ice. Some scientists say that this reduces their lifespan, as when their teeth wear out they can no longer keep their airholes open, and they die. It is certain that the Weddells have a shorter life expectancy than other seals so this could be the case. They live around the peninsula and in the Ross Sea area in the vicinity of McMurdo Sound.

If you lie on the frozen Sound and press your ear to the ice you can hear the Weddells calling to each other. It is an ancient song, ululant and ineffably sad. Similarly, during September Weddell cows are to be heard calling to each other on the surface of the ice as they struggle up through their holes at the end of winter to prepare for the birth of their pups. In the northern parts of their territory they pup as early as August, but in McMurdo Sound it happens towards the end of October. Pups weigh about 60lb at birth and the milk is so high in fat that they grow at an astonishing rate—as much as 5lb a day. The mothers shrink at the same rate. It is like watching dough rise and fall.

The **leopard seal** (*Hydrurga leptonyx*) is one of the penguin's greatest enemies, as it prowls through the pack ice looking for prey. It weighs less than the Weddell but is usually longer; it has a sleek body and a spotted underside. Leopards enjoy eating young crabeater seals too. The **crabeater** (*Lobodon carcinophagus*) is the most abundant seal in the world, its population probably exceeding 15 million—which means there are more crabeaters than all the other kinds of seal put together. The crabeater is as long as 8ft 6lb and as heavy as 500 pounds, but it does not eat crabs. It eats krill, and probably acquired the name as a result of confusion when the word was translated from a Scandinavian language. Crabeaters like to live in the pack ice, and you will see them either swimming or lounging on a floe—virtually never on land. They have light silvery bodies (the colour of the coat lightens in summer), a darker tail and flippers and a pointed snout. Pups are born in September, and suckle for about a month.

The **Ross seal** (*Ommatophoca rossi*) is about 6ft long and lives in the deep pack ice—one of the reasons why it is the least well known of all Antarctic seals. It was named after Sir James Clark Ross, who sailed south in the *Erebus* and *Terror* in the 19th century and collected two of his eponymous seals. Population estimates are about 220,000 (this is scientific guesswork). Although they live in the denser pack ice which means they are not so vulnerable to attack by killer whales and leopard seals, the Ross seal population is limited by the paucity of food available deep in the ocean.

The mighty **southern elephant seal** (*Mirounga leonina*, also known as the sea elephant), breeds on sub-Antarctic islands, and it is the largest seal. Bulls can get to 14½ft, and weigh four tons. They are dark grey, with a proboscis like a trunk, and are often grotesquely scarred as a result of fighting each other, particularly around the neck, and when their skin flakes off it looks like peeling wallpaper. They eat mainly squid, spiced up with some fish, and live most of the time in the water, assisted by a nice insulating layer of blubber (once highly sought after by human predators) as thick as six inches. They return to land to breed; well over a quarter of a million, for example, breed each year on South Georgia. The bulls preside over beach harems of 70 or more cows and a good deal of roaring goes on when the boss asserts his territorial rights. Elephant seal pups gain weight even more quickly than Weddells—as much as 9lb a day.

Birds

OK, so penguins are birds, but now I want to talk about the ones that can fly. Whilst there are no resident land birds, many genera, species and sub-species of seabird roam the Southern Ocean and the coastal fringes of Antarctica, and there is no room to list them all here, let alone describe them. Petrels, terns, prions, shags, gulls, sheathbills—these are just a few. But there is one which could not be left out of any list—the bird which features prominently in camp life wherever you are on the edge of Antarctica or on any sub-Antarctic island and surely the most unpopular creature in the south. I refer of course to the skua.

Skuas are predatory gulls. There are about six species, and they exist in north and south polar regions. The two most common types in the south are the south polar skua (*Catharacta maccormicki*, also known as McCormick's skua) and the slightly larger

Antarctic skua (*Catharacta antarctica*, also known as the brown skua) and in some areas a hybrid of the two exists. They look like fat brown pigeons, and often have white feathers in the wings, visible only when in flight. Sometimes their bodies are mottled. They have nastily pointed beaks and always look as if they are frowning. South polar skuas fly further south than the browns, although they leave the Antarctic in about May and travel north, returning in October in time to scoop up the Weddell seal placentas. They have a wingspan of over four feet, and the reason they are so unpopular is that they swoop down upon humans and take a swipe. On a short walk from a tent to a latrine you might get struck on the head a dozen times. The adults can weigh over 6lb so it is like being hit by a large frozen chicken hurled at great velocity. This is extremely unpleasant and although a wide range of defensive tactics have been invented over the years of human occupation, nothing really works except carrying a large pole above one's head and waving it about at all times. This is not a convenient strategy if one is trying to conduct a scientific experiment or enjoy a leisurely early-evening stroll. Skuas are a particular menace around penguin colonies and prey on both eggs and chicks (very young chicks can be gulped down whole). They can fly great distances, and on several occasions south polar skuas have been observed at the South Pole itself—a truly phenomenal achievement.

The legendary **albatrosses** enshrined by Samuel Taylor Coleridge in one of the greatest poems in the language (*see* p.20) are often observed wheeling above Antarctic waters. Sailors believed that killing an albatross brought ill luck. Most (but not all) species and sub-species of albatross circle above the Southern Ocean. They eat mainly squid, breed in colonies and can live to be as old as 50. The wandering albatross (*Diomedea exulans*) is the best known—over 40,000 pairs breed on South Georgia. The wanderer is the world's largest flying bird. Mainly white, with black and mottled black wings, it has a baby-pink bill and black eyes and can grow to 4½ft. Its wingspan often exceeds 11ft and it can fly at 50 miles an hour. The chicks are off-white, and become more snowy as they get older.

The black-browed albatross (*Diomedea melanophris*), popularly known as a mollymawk, breeds on sub-Antarctic islands and, like the larger wanderer, likes to follow ships. It is the most abundant and widely distributed of all albatrosses. The light-mantled sooty albatross (*Phoebetria palpebrata*) is half the size of the mighty wanderer and has a dark grey head shading into light grey around the neck and then into white.

ABOVE: *Skua gull.*
LEFT: *Wandering albatross, South Georgia.*

Actually, an albatross is a **petrel**. The name petrel covers many different 'tubenose' birds, but usually it refers to the smaller of the many species. The northern giant petrel (*Macronectes halli*) breeds on a number of sub-Antarctic islands and should not be confused with the southern giant petrel (*Macronectes giganteus*), also known as the Antarctic giant petrel, or stinker. Both have large bills. The southern version can be mottled black, white or grey, with a lighter underside than its northern counterpart, and it breeds on the Peninsula as well as sub-Antarctic islands, and sometimes on the continent itself. It has a reputation as a vicious scavenger and often preys on penguin chicks; it can be very distressing to see one hovering over a nest of stones until the penguin parent waddles off to sea to feed. The Antarctic petrel (*Thalassoica antarctica*) is much smaller than the Antarctic giant petrel (the names are confusingly similar). It has a dark brown head and back, most of the tail is white and the wings are half and half. It breeds on the other side of the continent to the mainly peninsular birds, in the Ross Sea area.

I think the snow petrel (*Pagodrama nivea*) is the most beautiful of all these birds. WIth its pure white feathers, black eyes and short black bill, as it glides among the bergs of the Southern Ocean it appears to be soaring through its own private symphony. Snow petrels live where there is pack ice, and breed on mountains or rocky hillocks all around the Antarctic continent. They are abundant, and can live as long as 20 years. Their wingspan is about 2½ft.

Unlike the snow petrel, storm petrels follow ships in bad weather. Wilson's storm petrel (*Oceanites oceanus*) is the most frequently observed storm petrel in Antarctic waters, and one of the most abundant seabirds in the world. It has been spotted at virtually every coastal base, as well as by passengers on most Southern Ocean cruisers. Contrary to mythology bandied around among Antarctic hands, it was not named after Edward Wilson, Scott's confidant, but after the 19th-century ornithologist Alexander Wilson. It is a delicate little bird weighing only a few ounces with a darkish brown body, a broad white band at the base of the tail, and a wingspan of about sixteen inches. The wings shade to a lighter brown towards the outside. Watching one of these creatures following a ship can be quite mesmerising—I have even found it hypnotic.

Prions are small birds of the Southern Ocean which feed on krill and plankton churned up by whales. They are blueish-grey, and some, for example the broad-billed prion

ABOVE: Southern giant petrel, white phase.
RIGHT: Grey-backed storm petrel, Falkland Islands.

(*Pachyptila vittata*), nest in burrows like certain petrels and shearwaters. Burrowing birds like these are therefore restricted to breeding grounds on sub-Antarctic islands, whereas larger petrels and other birds happily breed on a small cliff ledge. It's always worth scanning rock faces with binoculars. You may be rewarded by the sight of a solitary bird tending its fledglings.

Blue-eyed **shags** (*Phalacrocorax atriceps*, also known as Antarctic shags) live in colonies around the tip of the peninsula and on outlying islands. Nests are built with a mix of seaweed, moss and lichens. They breed further south than any other **cormorant** and are among the very few birds to remain in the Antarctic during the winter (the southern giant petrel is another). If you sail off the coast of the peninsula in a dinghy it is possible to scramble up lichen-clad rocks to see the dark-eyed chicks, almost as tall as their parents but cocoa-brown and fluffy. The adults have white fronts and black backs with long, smooth necks and eyes like blue marbles.

The Arctic **tern** (rejoicing in the Latin name *Sterna paradisaea*) is one of the most interesting of the forty tern species as it spends half the year in the Antarctic (the southern summer) and the other half—the northern summer—in the Arctic. Thus the bird enjoys almost perpetual daylight, and travels over 20,000 miles a year—one of the feats of the natural world. They look like Antarctic terns (*Sterna vittata*), with white bodies, black heads and red bills, except that the Antarctic ones have grey bands around the breast. The Antarctic tern stays where it is all year round, and nests on rocks in colonies near the coast.

Dominican gulls, sometimes called **kelp gulls,** have white bodies, black wings and yellow bills. They eat mainly limpets and appear on many islands and on the peninsula, usually competing for aeriel domination with the infernal skuas whose coarse cawing drowns them out.

Blue-eyed shag and chicks, Port Lockroy (gentoo penguin on nest).

The belt of water around the continent where the warm, salty currents from the tropics meet the colder and denser waters coming from the south is known as the Antarctic Convergence. This mixing creates an environment rich in nutrients, and a simple though highly effective food chain flourishes. At the bottom of this food chain, phytoplankton turns light into matter. Countless billions of animal plankton and other organisms find the waters of the Southern Ocean a conducive home—especially in the summer, when they enjoy constant light.

Such plankton constitute the diet of many thousands of other forms of life in the ocean. The most significant, by a wide margin, is the **krill**, a crustacean much like a shrimp. Of the krill species, *Euphausia superba*, one of the largest, is by far the most abundant in the Southern Ocean. It grows to a maximum length of two and a half inches, though there are so many of them that the biomass runs to many hundreds of millions of tons. Krill trawl around in vast shoals, sometimes miles wide, all changing direction at the same time, like synchronised swimmers. If you sail through the Southern Ocean you can see great pink blankets of them just below the surface (this is a good indication that whales may be in the vicinity). The amount of krill consumed by other marine creatures can barely be comprehended. Almost everything eats it, from fish to filter-feeding (baleen) whales. Humans beings can eat it too, and some nations, including the Japanese, have harvested krill from the Southern Ocean. Nobody has yet managed to breed it in captivity.

A variety of other marine invertebrates flourish, and on sub-Antarctic islands these are often visible on ice-free beaches. At least 20 species of **squid** are abundant in southern waters and they play an important part in the food chain, eaten in large numbers by some whales, seals, penguins and birds. The large ones can have mantle lengths in excess of 24ft. The real giants live in very deep waters, and as a result they are difficult to study.

Fish are less vital than squid in the Antarctic marine ecosystem, but they are still important. Many species of fish live happily in cold southern waters; most are specially adapted to cope with the temperatures and do not exist elsewhere (they have low metabolic rates, for example.) Some of the fish swimming around in McMurdo Sound manufacture their own anti-freeze. Among the most common of these is the Antarctic cod (*Dissostichus mawsoni*) which lives 1500ft down in the spectral depths of the Sound. A cod can weigh up to 125lb and looks as ancient as the slime from which we all crawled. They have phenomenally small brains and their cheeks are delicious raw as sashimi. Some of the fish which live in slightly warmer Antarctic waters have no haemoglobin at all, and their blood is clear.

One of the most mysterious and certainly the most endlessly fascinating creature in the whole of the natural world is a friendly resident of Antarctic waters. I mean of course the whale. He has not always found the pack ice a peaceful home. Whalers played an important part in the discovery of Antarctica, especially after they had bled the Arctic dry. A group of Dundonians set out in 1892, their thoughts fixed on the riches waiting for them in the Southern Ocean. They were sharp in turning their attention to southern waters: the Falklands sector of the Antarctic is the richest whaling ground in the world. But in technique, the Scots had already been beaten by their Norwegian rivals. Their equipment was outmoded and they were looking for the wrong kind of whale: they wanted bone for umbrellas and corsets, but the market wanted oil, not least for munitions.

Whaling died out in Dundee before the Great War, and the *Terra Nova* was the last whaler ever built by Dundonians. But in Antarctica the trade took off in the first two decades of the 20th century after the Norwegian Carl Larsen founded Grytviken on South Georgia and floating whale factories were developed. The industry reached its peak in southern waters in the 1930s. Despite the mystique—an early participant called it 'the greatest chase which nature yieldeth'—whaling was one of the hardest trades, and it employed the hardest drinkers. Business dropped off dramatically during the Second World War when synthetic glycerin was developed and most of the fleet was sunk by German raiders. After a few dying spurts, the last whaling station on South Georgia closed in 1965.

The **southern right whale** (*Eubalaena australis*) was the most popular with the 19th-century whalers, as it is rich in oil and floats when killed. Hence its name, as it was the 'right' whale to catch. It can grow to 58ft, and to a weight of 100 tons. At the turn of the century there were few southern rights left, but they are making a comeback. The southern right is a baleen whale, which means it feeds by taking in vast quantities of water and filtering out the krill or small fish through plates of a horny keratin substance which hang from the roof of its great mouth. As these whales are not hunters, they do not need to be as streamlined as their toothed cousins. They feed on krill (sometimes consuming as much as four per cent of their own body weight in a day), and take little dives for 20 minutes or so in between even shorter bursts on the surface. They move north to southern South America in the austral winter.

Larger still—the largest animal ever to have lived—is the **blue whale** (*Balaenoptera musculus*), a krill-eater observed during the summer among the Antarctic pack ice. The blue can grow to a hundred feet, and weigh 150 tons. There are probably about a

Southern minke whale.

thousand left. Next largest to the blue in Antarctic waters is the **fin whale** (*Balaenoptera physalis*), which is abundant. The **minke** (*Balaenoptera acutorostrata*) is the smallest of the baleen whales in the south (perhaps 25ft), with a black shiny top and a white tummy. It is the only baleen which stays in southern waters during the winter.

The most famous of all whales is the **killer** (*Orcinus orca; right*). It is a toothed whale, unlike those mentioned above, and, like most of that kind, smaller than the baleen whales. Killers are about thirty feet long, coal black on the top and bright white underneath, with that very distinctive dorsal fin that strikes fear into the heart of the

Killer whale.

swimmer. They tend to cruise around in pods, on the lookout for penguins, seals and fish. They haven't eaten anyone in Antarctic waters as far as we know, but Scott's photographer Herbert Ponting made a great deal, in his book *The Great White South*, of an episode on an ice floe during which he was attacked by killers and escaped (allegedly) by the skin of his teeth.

Among the other whales trawling the Southern Ocean I must mention the **sperm** (*Physeter macrocephalus*) immortalised by Herman Melville in his epic whaling novel *Moby-Dick*. It is long (males are as long as fifty feet) with a sinister boxy head. Although the one in *Moby-Dick* is white, this is rare. Most are dark grey. Sperms, which are toothed, eat as much as a ton of food a day, and favour squid.

Finally, the **southern bottlenose** whale which looks much more like a dolphin than a whale. It is grey or white, and has a small dorsal fin near the tail. You often see them alongside ships.

Plants

Most of Antarctica is too cold to sustain terrestrial life. There is no water for the hardiest tree. The 0.4 per cent of the continent not permanently covered by ice, however, does support life in the form of mosses and lichens, and beyond the continent itself, on sub-Antarctic islands, other kinds of plants survive, though they tend to take a long time to grow. Scientists have discovered that certain species are expanding their ranges quite rapidly, possibly as a result of climatic change. In other words as the ice retreats it is creating a larger terrestrial environment for the future. This is especially true on the milder and wetter peninsula.

The simplest form of life is the **single-celled alga**, and several hundred species have been identified. Many grow on rocks near penguin colonies and others appear on snow like splashes of blood. As for **lichen**, biologists reckon that as many as 100 species grow on the peninsula. One of the most common is from a group—*Usnea*—found in the Scottish highlands. Lichen grow at very low temperatures, unlike most plants, and they can do it with little moisture and no soil. They can take the extra nourishment they need direct from rock. It does take a long time for a lichen to grow, however—it could be as little as a twentieth of an inch in a century. The most prolific lichen-growths in Antarctica occur on the western coast of the peninsula, which is more protected than the other side, and on a number of outlying islands in the arc reaching out from the top of the peninsula.

Mosses aren't quite as hardy as lichens; they do like a bit of soil. You can expect to see them around seabird colonies, as the ground is enriched with guano and nesting material.

Two species of flowering plant are found as far south as 68 degrees (but no further). In other words, only on the northern part of the peninsula, and in sheltered places. They are *Deschampsia antarctica*, usually called Antarctic hairgrass, and *Colobanthus quitensis*, or Antarctic pearlwort. They do not exactly flourish like specimens in Kew Gardens. The hairgrass looks just like its name suggests—a few wispy strands of green grass with a barely distinguishable bloom. But such things are precious in the far south.

If you are cruising around the shallow waters of the peninsula you will see a variety of **seaweed**, especially as you approach the shore in inflatable boats. The western coast is the most fertile seaweed territory, and there you will see branchy brown forests of *Desmarestia anceps* waving around underneath the surface.

Insects

As I said at the beginning of this chapter, the largest land animal in Antarctica is a wingless midge a quarter of an inch-ong named *Belgica antarctica*. There are mites and springtails (land invertebrates) measuring slightly less, and again, the community is characterised by a multiplicity of individuals and few species. There are probably 15 to 20 species of insect at any one site but there could be millions of insects per square yard. None of these creatures have wings. They are mostly soil invertebrates so live in soil under rocks and stones and among lichens; if you dig around, you can see them. You will see springtails in particular around penguin colonies. They are black and shiny, and jump around a lot, like fleas. Generally they live only in reasonably damp areas with a bit of vegetation. They don't freeze in the winter, though everything around them freezes, as most of them accumulate anti-freeze in their cells. It is a substance close to glycol, like the stuff we put in our car radiators at the onset of winter. The water all around the animals might freeze, but as long as the fluid inside their cells doesn't, and the cells remain whole, a lot of the animals survive the winter

Besides these mites and springtails, visible with the naked eye (if you look hard), the warmer, ice-free zones of the Antarctic continent sustain communities of micro-organisms hiding in the rock. In the Convoy Range in the Dry Valleys on the fringes of the continent opposite Ross Island, for example, the sandstone turrets house crypto-endolithic micro-organisms which deep freeze in the winter. Like desert creatures, they have the ability to suspend life.

How to Approach Wildlife

- never touch the animals
- maintain a distance of at least 15ft from penguins, all nesting birds and most seals, and 50ft from fur seals
- give animals the right of way
- do not position yourself between a marine animal and its path to the water, or between a parent and its young
- always be aware of your surroundings; stay outside the periphery of bird rookeries and seal colonies
- keep noise to a minimum
- do not feed the animals, either ashore or from a ship
- most Antarctic species exhibit a lack of fear which allows you to approach relatively close; however, remember that the austral summer is a time for courting, mating, nesting, rearing young and moulting. If any animal changes or stops its activities upon your approach, you are too close. Be especially careful when taking photographs, since it is easy not to notice adverse reactions of animals when concentrating through the lens of a camera. Disturbing nesting birds may cause them to expose their eggs or offspring to predators or cold. Maintain a low profile, since animals can be intimidated by people standing over them. The disturbance of some animals, notably fur seals and nesting skuas, may elicit an aggressive, even dangerous, response.

Protecting Fragile Plants

- Antarctic lichens, mosses and grasses have very slow growth rates and damage from human activity can last decades. Tread carefully.

These guidelines were prepared by IAATO (the International Association of Antarctica Tour Operators).

ABOVE: *Mount Erebus by day. In the foreground is the frozen McMurdo Sound.*
BELOW: *The Transantarctic Mountains.*
TOP LEFT: *Mount Erebus as dawn breaks.*
BOTTOM LEFT: *Sculpted configurations of ice appear everywhere in Antarctica.*

Signpost at Terra Nova Bay, the headquarters of the Italian Antarctic programme

Geopolitics

Nobody indisputably owns Antarctica. Unlike anywhere else on the planet, any one individual has as much right to be there as any other. Although seven countries claim a sector of the continent, in practice their declarations of ownership don't mean much while the Antarctic Treaty is in force. The seven claimants are Britain, New Zealand, Norway, Chile, Argentina, Australia and France, and in one case—that of Chile, Argentina and Great Britain—the territory they claim overlaps, which just goes to prove what a conundrum the concept of Antarctic ownership really is.

Britain began making claims in the region almost two hundred years ago. Not surprisingly, at an early juncture its representatives decided that the bit they wanted was the Antarctic Peninsula, the wonky finger sticking out of the top left-hand corner of the continent—the most accessible, the earliest discovered and therefore always the most contentious part (the shortest distance between the continent and any other large landmass is the section of the Southern Ocean between the peninsula and South America). In 1820 Edward Bransfield claimed the South Shetland Islands for Britain, and in 1908 and 1917 Letters Patent were issued confirming these assertions. In 1920, when British Antarctic policy had begun to assume a coherent shape, the Under-Secretary of State at the British Colonial Office formally proposed that Britain should take over the whole continent for the Empire. Neither he nor anyone else knew what it was that they would be acquiring, even to the nearest million square miles; but they knew they wanted it.

By the 1930s a number of other nations were scrabbling around the peninsula. In 1948 the Argentinian, Chilean and British governments sent warships south in order to assert their 'rights' over a few thousand miles of ice. Arms were drawn by the Argentinians only in 1952 when they machine-gunfired on a British party, but feelings consistently ran very high indeed. After the war, Europeans were still optimistic that the continent could be made to earn its keep and as a result various crackpot schemes were put forward for its use as an enormous deep-freeze to stockpile grain.

The British Antarctic Survey now exists as a scientific research body under the auspices of the government-funded National Environment Research Council. For years its budget was eroded as the public purse came under increasing pressure. During the Falklands War in 1982, however, members of the House of Lords voiced the concern that the conflict might spread to what is quaintly known as 'British Antarctic Territory'. As a result, in 1983–4 BAS funding rose by more than sixty per cent.

Sovereign Claims in the Antarctic Treaty Region

National territories defined south of 60°S in the year after the
Antarctic Treaty came into force (1962).

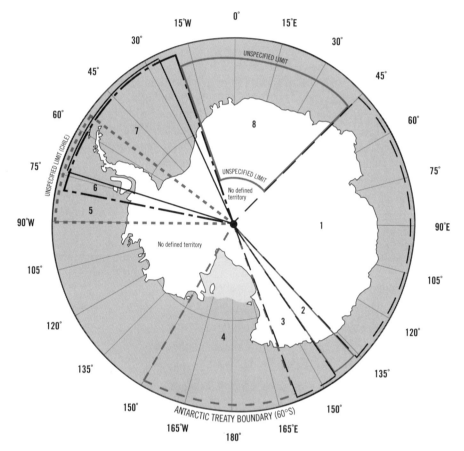

1. Australian Antarctic Territory (west sector) (45°E to 136°E, 60°S)

2. Terre Adélie (France) (136°E to 142°E, 60°S)

3. Australian Antarctic Territory (east sector) (142°E to 160°E, 60°S)

4. Ross Dependency (New Zealand) (150°W to 160°E, 60°S)

5. Territorio Antártico Chileno (53°W to 90°W, northern limit unspecified)

6. British Antarctic Territory (20°W to 80°W, 60°S)

7. Antártida Argentina (25°W to 74°W, 60°S)

8. Dronning Maud Land (Norway) (45°E to 20°W, northern limit unspecified)

Information supplied by R. K. Headland, Scott Polar Research Institute

109

The Antarctic Treaty

The Antarctic Treaty neither endorses nor refutes the claims of the seven nations. This international agreement, which came into force in 1961, evolved to preserve the fragile balance of ownership and non-ownership and to protect *Terra Incognita* from the depredations of exploitation and warfare and to make it a continent for science. Basically, the Treaty reserves Antarctica for peaceful scientific work. It states that 'Antarctica shall be used for peaceful measures only...in the interests of all humanity', and gives all parties free access to the whole of the continent, fostering science as the legitimate expression of national interest. Initiated during International Geophysical Year and applicable to all territory below 60°S, the Treaty was originally signed by 12 nations. Since then the number of signatories has more than tripled, reaching 43 in 1996. Any country may accede to the Treaty, but to have consultative status a nation must maintain a scientific involvement—which often means a base. The accession of India and Brazil in 1983, and China two years later, meant that the Treaty was no longer the exclusive territory of rich, developed nations. The document itself has also subsequently expanded.

The seven claimants, while adhering to the Treaty, still pursue the illusion that they have a special relationship with the continent. Several issue stamps at their Antarctic 'post offices' in order to reinforce the concept of territory. In practice, and in the minds of most other countries, ownership means nothing.

Major Provisions of the Antarctic Treaty

- *Antarctica is to be used for peaceful purposes only (although military personnel may be used for scientific purposes)*
- *Freedom of scientific investigation and cooperation*
- *Scientific data and personnel are freely exchanged*
- *Territorial claims are not recognized, disputed or established by the Treaty*
- *Nuclear explosions and radioactive waste disposal are banned*
- *All stations and equipment are open to inspection by any Treaty member*

The Seven Nations Claiming Antarctic Territory

- *Argentina*
- *Australia*
- *Chile*
- *France*
- *New Zealand*
- *Norway*
- *United Kingdom*

Bases

Over the past half-century well over 50 bases have been built in Antarctica. At present (1997) there are about 34 permanently manned stations. In addition, there are about 25 summer-only bases, and a couple of hundred huts intermittently occupied by scientists each summer. The population of Antarctica during the summer (October to February) is about 5000, and during the long dark winter it is about 1000. This gives a population density of one to every 5405 square miles.

According to the Treaty, all bases are open to inspection, and indeed inspection teams do visit their 'neighbours' from time to time to check on issues such as demilitarisation, environmental awareness and waste disposal. Although these visits are normally a formality resulting in little more than the exchange of lurid bottles of undrinkable liquor manufactured in the respective homelands of the station staff and the visiting inspection team, it does provide some kind of control mechanism.

Some of the Nations Represented in Antarctica

Australia

A pioneer of scientific research on the ice, Australia has maintained permanent stations in the subantarctic since 1947 and on the continent since 1954. It has the advantage of relative proximity: Hobart, the centre of Australian activities in the south, is closer to Antarctica than it is to Perth. Currently Australia has four permanent stations and maintains about a hundred people on the ice for 12-month stretches (about 400 more visit during the summer). Researchers from both government and university organisations conduct the scientific work, and Australian scientists have been particularly keen to investigate the seminal role of the Antarctic continent in the weather of the southern hemisphere. Australian National Antarctic Research Expeditions (ANARE) have recently launched a major strategic plan to remove rubbish that has accumulated on its bases over the years and to undertake environmental impact assessments. Its policy document also announces an intention to further develop its scientific record in the region through research in various fields, and to 'increase our influence within the Antarctic Treaty System based on the credibility of our research, the quality of our policies and our contribution to the management of the area.'

Italy

The Italian government signed the Antarctic Treaty in 1981. The country has subsequently developed an impressive, sophisticated and well-managed Antarctic research programme. The first Italian expedition set out in 1985, since when progress has been swift. A site for a station was immediately identified at Terra Nova Bay in Victoria Land so that Italy could claim consultative status to the Treaty, and Italian scientists began conducting experiments in the area. With the construction of Terra Nova Bay base, Italy was accepted as a full member of the Treaty in 1987. Now as many as fifty men and women work at Terra Nova each summer and the base has the reputation as the culinary centre of the continent—scientists from other nations regularly come up with spurious reasons for 'calling in' (if they can persuade anyone to fly them in) in order to sample the delights of a meal cooked by Ciro, the diminutive Neapolitan chef. Hercules aircraft from a Pisa-based squadron of the Italian airforce fly in to Terra Nova Bay from Christchurch until the ice runway melts (usually at the beginning of December), and then the scientists and support staff on base have to wait for the ship to arrive when the sea has fully melted. Terra Nova Bay remains a summer-only station.

New Zealand

The New Zealand base (Scott) is about the same size as Terra Nova Bay. Situated about two hundred miles away on Ross Island, the Kiwis keep a team of about ten people on the ice throughout the winter and as many as forty in summer. They are partly supported logistically by the much larger American base, McMurdo, over the hill. Unlike the Italians, however, the New Zealanders claim a portion of the continent, and they call this area the Ross Dependency.

The five major objectives of the country's involvement in Antarctica, as published in their policy document, are:

- *international collaboration in scientific research*
- *protection of the Antarctic environment*
- *preservation of peace in the region*
- *maintenance of the Antarctic Treaty*
- *enhancement of New Zealand's stewardship of the Ross Dependency*

Although the Kiwis only have one base, they operate field camps in the vicinity of Ross Island, notably at Lake Vanda in the Wright Valley on the Antarctic continent, where teams of hydrologists from New Zealand have been roaming for several decades. Whilst their scientific research is taken seriously, Kiwis are widely acknowledged to have the most fun on the ice, displaying the same amiability, *laissez-faire* attitudes and egalitarianism as they do at home.

Chile and Argentina

The bottom of South America—Tierra del Fuego down to Cape Horn, in other words—is only three hours away from the tip of the Antarctic peninsula in a Hercules plane, so it is perhaps not surprising that Chile and Argentina have a special relationship with the continent. Also they are young nations, with disputed border areas, and so the concept of territorial ownership is acutely felt at all levels of society and government. In order to bolster the notion that their little slices of the last continent are merely an extension of home, both the Chileans and the Argentinians make it as much like home as possible. Each has several bases. At the main Chilean base, situated on King George Island and called Teniente Rodolfo Marsh, there is a school, a hospital, a chapel and a bank. Some male workers and navy personnel bring their wives and children down to the ice with them on their tour of duty, and Radio Sovereign FM is broadcast from the weather station. General Pinochet flew down to King George Island in 1977 and declared that it was merely a continuation of Chilean territory. Six families were despatched there in 1984 to institute a 'permanent' settlement. On the other side of the Andes the entire Cabinet took off from Buenos Aires and landed on the ice to prove how very Argentinian it was.

Peru, Brazil and Uruguay

Other South American republics have also cast their eyes south. The Peruvians have named their base Machu Picchu. Brazil and Uruguay both maintain lively bases on King George Island.

Russia, China and Poland

The islands north of the peninsula are the most popular site for bases for many other nationalities besides South Americans, and this is understandable, as it costs everyone much less to get there and some of the land is not permanently ice-covered. King George Island, squatting in the archipelago named the South Shetlands by Scottish sealers, is an especially popular site for bases. The Russians are there, as are the Poles and the Chinese. The Chinese base is called Great Wall and displays an enormous painting of a panda on the side of a hilltop hut.

The Russians have a long and illustrious record in Antarctica, with many scientific firsts to their credit. Their base on King George Island, Bellingshausen, is far less remote than other Russian stations, notably Vostok, in East Antarctica, and the coastal Mirny. Vostok is actually situated at the South Geomagnetic Pole, and it is still supplied by a convoy of tractors from Mirny over 800 miles away.

Japan and India

Japan, an original signatory of the Antarctic Treaty, has been pursuing a vigorous programme for years. The second Asian country to sign up was India, which in 1983 became the first developing nation in Asia to become a full Treaty member. India's involvement in Antarctica had emerged largely as a result of prime minister Jawaharlal Nehru's vision in the fifties of his country's global position.

The United Kingdom

The British Antarctic Survey, which is headquartered in Cambridge, currently maintains four bases in Antarctica. The main one, Rothera, is on Adelaide Island off the Antarctic Peninsula, and it supports a winter population of twenty-one and a summer population of up to a hundred. Rothera has a crushed-rock airstrip and throughout the summer a DASH-7 plane ferries scientists between the base and the Falklands. Halley Base, the second largest, is much more remote. It stands on a floating ice shelf on the east coast of the Weddell Sea. The Halley relief operation is a major task, with supplies being landed by ship on to the ice shelf and then towed over seven miles to the base on sledges by Sno-Cat.

Halley is only visited once each year by a BAS ship, so everything that is needed for a whole year has to be put in on this one visit. Halley is a centre for upper atmospheric research and ice and climate studies, and it was here that measurements were made that demonstrated unequivocally the depletion of ozone in the stratosphere over Antarctica. Sixteen people winter at Halley and up to 70 live there in the summer.

Signy Island is a summer-only base in the South Orkneys (*see* **What to See**, p.51). Bird Island is the smallest BAS station, and the most northerly: it is situated off the western end of South Georgia, and on it scientists study penguin and seal population dynamics and undertake studies such as the satellite tagging of albatross. Eight people live at Bird Island during the summer and three or four in the winter. The base became famous in Antarctica when it was discovered that its residents had been participating for years in an international radio darts contest between bases without ever possessing a dart board.

For historical information about the British Antarctic Survey *see* **History**, pp.135–6.

The United States

The programme run by the United States outstrips any other in size and scope, though Russia isn't far behind. As many as 1200 people at any one time live at McMurdo, the main US base, during the summer. Financed and managed by the National Science Foundation, a government agency, and maintained by a private contractor based in Colorado, the US Antarctic Program has outgrown its naval origins. With a budget hovering just below $200 million, the Antarctic programme represents six per cent of the NSF budget. As the US Department of Defense has contracted, so the Navy (more properly, a joint military force) has been withdrawing from Antarctic operations, a process which looks set to continue.

The Americans have three stations on the continent. McMurdo, the largest, is on Ross Island, Palmer is near the peninsula, and at 90°S sits the showpiece of the US Antarctic Program: South Pole Station, called Amundsen-Scott. The decision to inaugurate an International Geophysical Year in 1957–8 encouraged the Americans to build up their Antarctic programme. In addition, the Soviets were known to be nurturing a desire to build a station at the Pole. When they learnt of this, the US government immediately passed a resolution that work should begin immediately on an American base at the South Pole—that way, the Soviets would be beaten to it. The competitive spirit was reminiscent of the race for space.

The station was completed in February 1957, and the Soviet Union established a base at the scientifically important South Geomagnetic Pole. In 1961 the Americans lost the space race when Yuri Gagarin went up on the first manned space flight.

Contrary to what many people believe, the United States does not maintain any designation of territory in Antarctica. The explanation for this position goes back much further than the Treaty. It began in 1924, when Secretary of State Charles Evans Hughes wrote that the discovery of lands unknown to civilization 'does not support a valid claim of sovereignty unless the discovery is followed by an actual settlement of the discovered country'. Roosevelt endorsed this notion with specific reference to Antarctica in 1939. US policy in Antarctica is based on four principles. The official version reads:

- *we recognize no foreign territorial claims*
- *we reserve the right to participate in any further uses of the region*
- *Antarctica shall be used for peaceful purposes only*
- *there shall be free access for scientific investigation and other peaceful pursuits*

Environmental Issues

Mining

While over-fishing is the most serious environmental issue in the waters of the Southern Ocean, the great danger perceived to be threatening the continent itself is exploitation of its oil and mineral reserves. These resources are known to be there, though it would be hellishly expensive to get them out from under all that ice. During the eighties, the strongly promoted fear that certain nations were going to start barging around misusing Antarctica as they have misused their own countries lay behind the setting up of an environmental protocol to the Antarctic Treaty. It was a complicated, deeply disputed and long-winded affair. A number of countries quickly signed the Treaty during that time so they could have a piece of the oil pie everyone thought might be up for grabs.

The Protocol on Environmental Protection was signed in Madrid in 1991. It imposed a 50-year moratorium on oil- and mineral-mining anywhere in Antarctica. This was a turning point in the history of the continent—though it took a long time for all the nations involved to ratify the Protocol, and at the beginning of 1997 it was still not actually in force.

Under the terms of the original Treaty, then, weapons testing, nuclear explosions and the disposal of radioactive waste are forbidden. Various other agreements have been negotiated and ratified within what is known as the 'Treaty System', for example the Convention on the Conservation of Antarctic Marine Living Resources (CCAMLR), which protects fish in waters south of the Antarctic Convergence (the belt of water at about 50°S where the waters of the Atlantic, Pacific and Indian Oceans mix).

Representatives of Treaty signatories gather annually in the capital cities of member nations to discuss matters relating to Antarctica and decide how it will be run. Non-governmental environment organisations are observers at most Treaty meetings through the Antarctic and Southern Ocean Coalition (ASOC), which is an international umbrella organisation for about 200 groups including Greenpeace. Some of these NGOs have a vision for Antarctica. They want it to be declared a World Park for perpetuity. Greenpeace and other environmental groups have been lobbying hard for this (Greenpeace has claimed responsibility for significant improvements in the scope of legislation protecting Antarctica, and the claim has some justification, but many of the clean-up operations are a consequence of increasing tourism). According to the environmental lobby, Antarctica—the last wilderness—should be free from international competition and *never* mined or exploited.

In 1991 Treaty signatories agreed to designate the continent 'a natural reserve devoted to peace and science'.

Greenpeace has put forward the argument that international co-operation within a World Park framework could:

- *ensure minimal duplication of facilities and research*
- *enable the development of a long-term, international plan for the future of science in Antarctica*
- *enhance the quality of scientific research and value for money of Antarctic activities*
- *minimise the number of personnel in Antarctica, thus reducing the amount of fuel used, and of waste and sewage generated*
- *minimise unnecessary impacts and threats to the environment*

Everyone is aware of the need to protect Antarctica. Ros Kelly, Australian Minister for the Arts, Sport, the Environment, Tourism and Territories, said this: 'Conserving this greatest wilderness is an awesome responsibility, yet to do so is vital not only for science but also for the future of the whole planet.'

The Agreed Measures for the Conservation of Antarctic Flora and Fauna of 1978 governs the removal of flora and fauna, restricts the use of designated pollutants and legislates for the series of protected areas set up to preserve wildlife. These are called Sites of Special Scientific Interest, or SSSIs, and cannot be built on or worked within without permission from the regulatory body. A permit system enables scientists to collect specimens and enter protected areas if they have a compelling scientific purpose. The system provides for public comment on each permit application. Penguin colonies are often designated SSSIs.

Although the geopolitics of Antarctica are complex, scientific information is shared. To facilitate this, all programmes are required to submit descriptions of their science projects to an international Antarctic science body called the Scientific Committee on Antarctic Research (SCAR), ostensibly so research data is freely available and as a result not wastefully duplicated. There are many examples of the fruitful exchange of information in Antarctica. Faraday, for example, for many decades an important British meteorological station on the peninsula and since 1996 run by the Ukrainians and renamed Vernadsky, collects weather data from the British, American and German bases on that side of the continent and sends it to the Chilean station Teniente Rodolfo Marsh. The Chileans collate this with data from South American stations and send it all on to the World Meteorological Organisation database.

Other Environmental Issues

One of the objectives of the Treaty is to ensure that national programmes take a responsible attitude towards waste disposal. Before this happened, many hundreds of tons of waste had been left behind, many fuel spills had contaminated the ice and the US programme had even installed a 1.8 megawatt nuclear reactor at McMurdo station. In the good old days, veterans recall that if people wanted to get rid of things like irretrievably broken caterpillar trucks, they would tow them out on to the sea ice and leave them there until the ice melted and they sank.

Sophisticated post-Treaty waste-management programmes have evolved—though they are more scrupulously adhered to by some countries than others—and a great deal of time and money is spent on ensuring that waste is properly collected, compacted and, usually, returned to 'the real world'. In pristine areas such as the Dry Valleys opposite Ross Island, even urine and washing-up water is flown out so as not to upset the delicate balance of the ecosystem. Dumping has been outlawed by most countries. Open burning has been stopped at the majority of stations and according to the provisions of the Treaty it must be phased out everywhere by the end of the 1998/9 season. The Treaty permits incineration, but only on the understanding that incinerators must to the maximum extent practicable reduce harmful emissions. Recommendations do prohibit the incineration of specifically harmful substances such as rubber and pvc.

The problem with much of this legislation, clearly, is that it is open to interpretation. To ask someone to do something 'to the maximum extent practicable' is surely holding a hostage to fortune. In addition, most of the time no one is around to see what's going on. As long as you get rid of the evidence before the next inspection team arrives—which could be years, if you are at a remote site—you can, effectively, do anything you like.

As Antarctic programmes mature, change shape or run out of money, bases are often abandoned. This still causes serious environmental problems, despite the fact that the Environmental Protocol to the Treaty stipulates that all Antarctic programmes must remove their debris. Once huts and machinery become frozen into the ice, for example, they are a hazard to penguins, seals and birds. Fuel drums leak. Greenpeace has been struggling to bring this issue to the world's attention for some time, and in 1995 estimated that over 35 abandoned bases and facilities required cleaning up. During an inspection of the abandoned González Videla base, belonging to Chile, representatives from Greenpeace counted 100 fuel drums, 14 of them leaking heavy lubrication oil through gentoo penguin nests into the sea. (The Chilean government has recently undertaken a major clean-up at González Videla.)

The construction of landing facilities for aircraft is also a contentious issue, with arguments frequently raging between environmental pressure groups and national Antarctic programmes. The disruption of wildlife is the main bone of this contention. The biggest scrap took place in the 1980s over the 3300ft hard rock airstrip at the French Dumont d'Urville base at Pointe Géologie. Two summers of dynamiting disrupted the rich bird life and interfered with breeding grounds.

It is not permitted to bring animals into Antarctica. In theory at least the last has been seen of the expedition cats which the men of Scott's day wrote about so fondly in their diaries (see **Living in Antarctica**, p.78, for information about the huskies). The rationale behind this is the protection of indigenous wildlife. Inspection teams are always on the alert for domesticated wildlife—in other words the station's pet skua or penguin—as the Protocol does not permit the feeding of scraps to animals or birds lest diseases are transmitted. All very admirable, but it is less than human to expect a small group of men and women suffering severe sensory deprivation to refrain from making friends with the creatures they see around them. In practice too, a number of stations do have pet cats...

As the US programme is the largest in Antarctica it is hardly surprising that it has the most developed waste-management systems. The National Science Foundation requires every scientist going south to analyse the environmental impact of his or her project. More than 120 specific environmental documents (these are public) have been issued by the Office of Polar Programs. Trained observers are carried aboard selected tourist ships as part of a voluntary system to make sure US citizens comply with the environmental standards of the Antarctic Conservation Act (you might bear this in mind as you stick your chewing gum under your deckchair). Fuel handling has recently been improved at McMurdo by replacing rubber bladder tanks with double-walled steel tanks. At the South Pole station all open-trench disposal of solid waste has stopped, and the station now sends all its solid waste to McMurdo for processing (this of course is horrendously expensive, and burns hundreds of gallons of fuel, especially as the planes which take the stuff out land on skis and so have reduced cargo capacity...)

Almost all bases on the continent require you to sort your rubbish before throwing it into a bin. Everyone says that when they get back home they find themselves standing in the kitchen with a tin can in their hand thinking, 'Now, which bin does this go in?' In the case of the American programme there are so many categories to choose from that life can get very complicated indeed. Take a tube of Pringles potato crisps. The lid is Light Metal—or is it Aluminium, which is a separate category? The tube is Cardboard—or Food Contaminated, since the crisps have been in it? On the other hand, of course, it could be Domestic Combustibles. In any event, you had better rip off that metal rim around the bottom, as that will have to go in a separate category. Perhaps you should peel off the paper coating glued to the cardboard tube, too. And if there are any crisps left inside, they will have to go in Food Waste... It can take a while to empty a black plastic rubbish sack from your tent once you get back to base. At McMurdo the waste-management people have set up a hotline on the station telephone network so you can ring up and have someone talk though the process for disposing of a Pringles tube.

As for smoking, some bases are like offices in Manhattan: smokers can be seen huddling together outside the door. This is bad news in a blizzard. And if you ever dare throw a cigarette butt down on the ice you're in big trouble.

In the end, though, geopolitics dwells in the north. On the ice there is only one enemy: the cold.

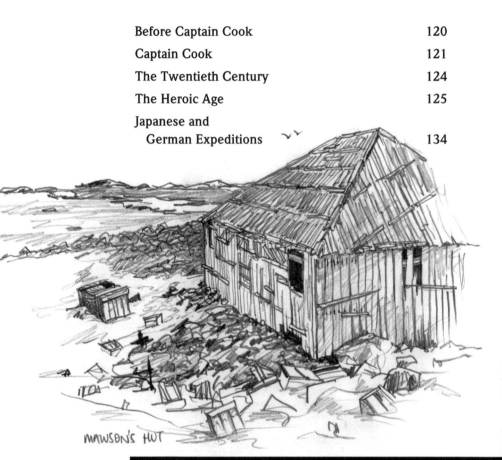

MAWSON'S HUT

History

Speculation about a possible continent at the southern axis of the globe was drifting around learned circles and occupying the minds of great thinkers as early as several hundred years before Christ. Until the 19th century, however, nobody really had any idea what was down there. When my grandmother was born, in 1901, the streets of London were lit by gaslight, Queen Victoria was dead and Roosevelt was in the White House, but hardly any of Antarctica was even mapped. Indeed, until the 18th century it was widely believed that there might be people living on a southern continent, grazing their flocks on abundant verdant pastures. For most of what we call 'history', Antarctica was a Shangri-la, a mythical space of the imagination.

Before Captain Cook

As far as we know, the Ancient Greeks were the first to suspect that there might be a great southern landmass at the bottom of the world. Texts have survived which show that it was discussed in the marketplace of Athens during the 4th century BC: men looked at the winds and the oceans and *sensed* that Antarctica was there. They were familiar with the bright clusters of stars in the north, and had named them Arktos, the bear. Conceiving as they did of a balance in nature, they decided that the Arktos must therefore be balanced by an Anti Arktos—'opposite the bear'—in the south.

In AD 150 Ptolemy drew a continent on his map called *Terra Australis Incognita*, the 'Unknown Southern Land', and the existence of an Antarctica became fixed in the collective geographic mind. Over a thousand years were to pass before the Portuguese navigator **Ferdinand Magellan** sailed around the islands of Tierra del Fuego at the tip of South America in 1520, saw fires burning on the shore and realised that the territory was populated. This fuelled the notion of a great land still further to the south, for if people lived that far down, why not further?

Fifty-eight years later, however, **Francis Drake** sailed round Cape Horn and declared there was nothing beyond it. He could see the union of the Pacific and the Atlantic, and so thought all the land must have petered out. None the less, Plancius's *Planisphere*, published in 1592, shows both the Antarctic continent and *circulus antarcticus*. Plancius, Mercator and the other cartographers struggling to make sense of it all interpreted medieval theory in the light of Spanish and Portuguese voyages. They decided, on at best flimsy evidence, that this land must be very big, mightily hard of access—and populated. On the examples of their work that have survived, Antarctica appears in all kinds of bulbous shapes and unfamiliar sizes. It was the ultimate cartographic stab in the dark, even in an age when the global map was still very sketchily drawn.

As more pioneering spirits ventured south in their creaky ships, cartographers were kept busy lopping off bits of Antarctica which didn't exist. Seafarers charted subantarctic islands which they surmised were the great southern land, but until the late 18th century nobody really had the first practical idea what, if anything, was down there.

Captain Cook

Captain James Cook revolutionised man's knowledge of the Southern Ocean and began the long, slow process of discovery that was to result in the last tracts of the Antarctic ice-fields being mapped by satellite in the 1960s. Cook's second voyage made all the Antarctic exploration which had gone before him look insignificant.

On his three great Pacific voyages Cook charted the whole ocean, and he did it so accurately that his charts can still be used today. He set out in 1768 in the *Endeavour* on an expedition organised by the Royal Society and recorded the transit of Venus over the disc of the sun from Tahiti. He then proved there was no land to the south and west of Tahiti and became the first white man to reach the east coasts of New Zealand and Australia. On the second voyage, in 1772, he was under Admiralty instructions to find the great southern land. He had always suspected that there was no such thing, despite the fact that the weight of the scientific establishment at home pressed upon its existence. Opinion was greatly divided, even aboard the *Resolution* and its sister ship the *Adventure*.

Cook was a Yorkshireman with little formal education, and he worked on the Whitby coal-carriers before signing up with the Navy and applying himself to the cutting edge of 18th-century science. He was measured and always had his finger on the pulse of his men, who were frequently drunk. Cook took care to learn from those who had gone before him, and, unlike the crews battling around Antarctica over a century later, Cook's men never got scurvy, a potentially deadly disease caused by a chronic lack of vitamin C.

On 17 January 1773, aboard *Resolution*, he reached 66½°S and crossed the Antarctic Circle, the first man to do so. He then discovered the circumpolarity of the Southern Ocean. In January 1775 he claimed South Georgia, though he wasn't impressed with the island, writing in his journal that the land he had seen was 'a country doomed by nature never once to feel the warmth of the sun's rays, but to lie buried under everlasting snow and ice, whose horrible and savage aspect I have not words to describe.' Cook discovered that there could be no people there after all; it was too cold. The myth died. As he sailed away he concluded 'there is not the least room for the possibility of there being a continent, unless near the Pole and out of reach of navigation... Should anyone possess the resolution and the fortitude to elucidate this point by pushing yet further south than I have done, I shall not envy him the fame of his discovery, but I make bold to declare that the world will derive no benefit from it.' Four years later this great man, only fifty years old, was stabbed to death with an iron dagger in the waters of Kealakekua Bay in Hawaii.

Cook had married in 1762, and his widow Elizabeth survived him by 56 years. Like most sailors' wives, she had been forced to accept the fact that she was destined to spend most of her married life apart from her husband. James and Elizabeth enjoyed a total of about four years together. What a lonely life it must have been for the explorers' wives left behind. Elizabeth Cook's destiny was especially tragic. Before her husband's death she lost two children in infancy. Then, after Cook's murder, her three surviving sons died. Two of them had followed in their fathers' footsteps and joined the Navy, and they were lost at sea.

Still, Elizabeth made the most of her life. She had a dinner party every Thursday at three o'clock, and often spoke of her husband, though always as 'Mr Cook'. She never called him 'Captain'.

Navigators and explorers from other nations were active in southern waters in Cook's era, but none had his success. In 1771, the year before the 462-ton wooden *Resolution* sailed out of Sheerness under Captain Cook, **Yves-Joseph de Kerguélen-Trémarec** had left France with instructions from the king to proceed to Mauritius and from there sail south in search of the southern continent. He sighted land at 50°S and named it South France—but it turned out to be a group of inhospitable rocky islands.

Sealers and Whalers

Sealers and whalers came after Captain Cook. Besides the fact that the seal population of the northern hemisphere was beginning to dwindle thanks to the exhaustive depredations of the hunters, an Englishman called **William Smith** was partly responsible for initiating this flurry of activity. He was sailing around Cape Horn in 1819 on the Argentina–Chile trade route, and was driven south by the kind of inclement weather for which the Cape is renowned. He was so tantalised by the glimpses of snow, ice and—who knows?—perhaps a continent that he returned the following season, without cargo, to investigate. On his third trip he landed on islands strung out like a rosary northwest of the Antarctic Peninsula, and named them the South Shetlands. This group covers 335 miles from the first rocky rosary bead to the last, and it constitutes the largest archipelago in the Antarctic regions. Williams sailed home and reported enormous quantities of seals.

The sealers came, all right: they almost wiped out the fur seals around South Georgia and the South Shetland Islands, and continued to exploit those of all the peri-Antarctic islands.

First Sightings

The Antarctic continent probably wasn't sighted until 1820, and it was almost certainly **Fabien Bellingshausen**, an Estonian commanding a Russian expedition, who saw it first, on 20 January. Tsar Alexander I was in an expansionist frame of mind, and he despatched expeditions to both polar regions, north and south. Bellingshausen, who was born the year Cook died, became a captain in the Imperial Russian Navy and a fine explorer. He had competition in the Southern Ocean, however. The American sealer **Nathaniel Palmer** was 21 when, in 1820, he rang the bell of his small ship *Hero* in thick fog off the coast of the South Shetland Islands. He thought he was hundreds of miles from another ship, and then he heard a bell clanging in reply. It was from Bellingshausen's ship, the *Vostok*. The two took tea together (or it might have been a slug of vodka). Palmer claimed to have seen the continent, as did the British **Edward Bransfield** (who had William Smith aboard).

First Landings

It seems reasonably certain that sealers were the first to land on the Antarctic continent. The American sealing master **John Davis** landed on the peninsula from the shallop *Cecilia* on 7 February 1821, and **John McFarlane** aboard *Dragon* which had sailed from London landed at an unknown date that same season. It is virtually certain that other continental landings took place, but as the crews didn't find any fur seals on the peninsula they quickly went elsewhere in search of their quarry.

The assertion that the explorer Carsten Borchgrevink made the first landing on the continent in 1895 is one of the more commonly repeated fallacies of Antarctic history (see later in this chapter for information about Borchgrevink's subsequent expedition).

Weddell, Biscoe, Dumont d'Urville and Wilkes

Not long after these first sightings, in 1823, **James Weddell**, a sealing captain in command of the *Jane*, sailed to a latitude of 74°S in the sea now named after him—the furthest south ever reached by man. He had another ship with him, the *Beaufoy*, and both were looking for fur seals. The most prolific seal in Antarctica is named after Weddell.

John Biscoe arrived south in command of a ship sent out by the Enderby Brothers of London (also Weddell's sponsors). He came down from South America, sailed east from the South Shetlands in 1831 and crossed the Antarctic Circle. Biscoe made some discoveries, and bestowed the name of Sir James R.G. Graham, then First Lord of the Admiralty, upon the Antarctic Peninsula. Others were sailing around at this time, sniffing for land, notably **Jules Dumont d'Urville**, a French navy captain who led an expedition in 1838 on the frigates *Astrolabe* and *Zélée*. He made discoveries around the north of the peninsula and named both a species of penguin and a chunk of land after his wife, Adélie.

In 1838 **Charles Wilkes** of the US Navy took five ships down to the ice on the United States Exploring Expedition with instructions to follow Weddell's route as far as possible, journey to the most southerly point reached by Cook and try to cross the Antarctic Circle south of Tasmania. One ship sank, one was sent home early, one was sold and a fourth hit a berg. Wilkes failed to reach Cook's southernmost point, and did not cross the Antarctic Circle either. He made some discoveries, some of which have subsequently been disproved. When he got back to America in 1842 he was much criticised for poor leadership, and a shadow descended over his career and his reputation.

James Clark Ross

James Clark Ross crossed the Antarctic Circle and penetrated the sea which now bears his name during a Royal Navy voyage he led between 1839 and 1843. Ross joined up when he was eleven, went off to the Arctic with his uncle to look for the Northwest Passage, the geographical grail of its day, became a scientist and located the North Magnetic Pole (the north pole of the earth's magnetic field, as opposed to the geographic North Pole, which is the northern point of the earth's rotation). He wanted to find the South Magnetic Pole as well and achieve a kind of polar double whammy, but didn't. He set out in two specially strengthened warships, *Erebus* and *Terror*, and in them discovered great swathes of the ice edge, including what is now known as the Ross Ice Shelf. His crews were the first to see the active volcano he named Mount Erebus after his ship. Names were bestowed by

Ross up and down the section of the Antarctic coast he discovered—Mount Terror on Ross Island was named after his second ship; Cape Crozier on the same island after his best friend **Francis Crozier**, captain of the Terror; and McMurdo Sound, which has since given its name to the main American base on the continent, after the same ship's first lieutenant, **Archibald McMurdo**. Ross spent more than four years in the south, and when he returned to England he was knighted by Queen Victoria.

After his return from the south Ross married—though only after he had signed an agreement with his fiancée's father that there would be no more polar voyages.

Wintering in the Pack Ice—and on the Continent

Once again, after Ross, the veil descended. In 1873 the British warship HMS *Challenger* was converted into a floating laboratory and despatched south to see if it could throw any light on the matter. It was the first steamship to cross the Antarctic Circle. Scientists pulled up rocks from the seabed which they reckoned came from a continent, but the expedition added precious little to the map.

In 1898 the crew of the *Belgica* became the first to winter in the southern pack ice. They were under the command of **Captain Adrien de Gerlache** of the Belgian Navy. Seven nationalities were represented on board. The Norwegian **Roald Amundsen** was on this expedition, and so was **Frederick Cook**, the American who later claimed to be the first to reach the North Pole. The ship was not properly equipped, and the long, dark months of the polar night were wretched. When a lieutenant died, it almost broke their spirit. Many showed symptoms of scurvy. The expedition discovered some islands, but the crew paid a high price.

Carsten Borchgrevink led the first expedition to winter on the continent itself in 1898, aboard the *Southern Cross*. Although it was called the British Antarctic Expedition, all but five of its members were Norwegian. Borchgrevink was a naturalised Australian whose father was Norwegian, and the British geographical establishment of the day balked at this intrusion on what they considered their territory. Borchegrevink had high hopes. He wrote, 'The Antarctic may be another Klondike...there are fish—fisheries might be established...here is quartz in which metals are to be seen.' As with so many expeditions, the men who were supposed to be setting an example—in this case Borchgrevink and one of his chief scientists, the Australian physicist Louis Bernacchi— quarrelled bitterly. Still, they enjoyed spectacular successes sledging with the dogs (they were the first to take dogs).

The Twentieth Century

Otto Nordenskjöld led a Swedish scientific expedition in the *Antarctic*, and reached the peninsula in 1902. After one winter the ship was crushed by the pack ice of the Weddell Sea while Nordenskjöld and five men were on an island several days sailing away. They spent two years waiting to be picked up. The twenty crew who were aboard escaped on floes and wintered again in a stone hut on a small island. A third group were elsewhere, also waiting for a ship which never came. Amazingly, all three groups met up. This must go down in history as one of the most serendipitous meetings of all time. Only one man died on the expedition, and he was buried on Paulet Island, but everyone else was rescued in 1904 by an Argentinian relief ship, one of three expeditions sent to the rescue.

News that the Swedes were in difficulty had spread, however, and in 1903 French scientist **Jean-Baptiste Charcot**, who had been planning an expedition to the Arctic, changed his mind and took his own ship, the *Français*, south. He also wanted to find out, among other things, if Antarctica was a continent or a series of large islands.

At that time five national expeditions were exploring Antarctic waters: German, Swedish, British, Scottish and French. Charcot heard that the Swedes were safe before he got to the pack ice, but he proceeded, wintered, crossed the Antarctic Circle and explored the peninsula. Having returned to France the lure of the south pulled him back, as it has pulled so many, and he returned in 1908 in a far more sophisticated ship called the *Pourquoi Pas?* (Why Not?). Again he and his crew wintered and carried out peninsular exploration.

William Spiers Bruce led the Scottish National Antarctic Expedition to the Weddell Sea area in 1902–4. He took a relatively large number of scientists, conducted oceanographical investigations and established a meteorological station on the South Orkneys (it was subsequently transferred to the Argentinians). The team spent a winter on Laurie Island in the South Orkneys, and discovered Coats Land, which they named after the expedition's chief sponsor.

The Heroic Age

Things were clearly hotting up in the south. Why were so many men driven to risk so much and endure such hardships? It was the possibility of financial gain, for some, as they hoped they might find minerals. For others it was national prestige—nobody wanted to be left out of the only unknown and unowned segment of the globe. And of course, as the climber George Mallory is famous for saying about Everest but probably never did, it was because it was there. Scott's geologist on his second expedition, Frank Debenham, wrote 'Man strives for complete knowledge of his world just as a small boy climbs an apple tree even if there is no apple at the top.'

There was another reason. After all those long, hard centuries, man had attained the most alluring geographical goal on earth: he had reached the North Pole—or so it was thought at the time. In 1909 two Americans, Robert Peary and Frederick Cook, separately claimed to have reached the North Pole. Just as people tired of the moon after 1969, eyes sated on the north turned in another direction. They looked south.

Polar historians have coined the phrase 'the Heroic Age' to describe the short burst of epic expeditions and sledging journeys in the first two decades of the twentieth century. The four main protagonists of this period are Robert Falcon Scott, who was English, the Anglo-Irish Ernest Shackleton, Norwegian Roald Amundsen and British-born Australian Douglas Mawson. The Heroic Age is usually reckoned to date from Scott's first expedition to the death of Shackleton, but to be more accurate it began at the Sixth International Geographical Congress at London's Imperial Institute in 1895. On 3 August those present passed a resolution 'that this Congress record its opinion that the exploration of the Antarctic regions is the greatest piece of geographical exploration still to be undertaken', and went on to urge scientific societies throughout the world to start planning.

Captain Scott

Scott, an officer in the Royal Navy, led two expeditions, setting out first in 1901 in the specially commissioned 700-ton *Discovery* supported by the Royal Geographical Society and financed by both private and public funds. He went down to the Ross Sea, cruised along the Ross Ice Shelf, then called the Barrier, almost as far as 150 degrees west, and discovered land of a continental character which he named King Edward VII Land. Scott's chief scientist was Edward 'Bill' Wilson, an accomplished doctor, naturalist and artist. The two men were great friends, and Scott relied on Wilson's advice a good deal. The *Discovery* scientists sent a balloon up to get a better view. Scott went up in it first. It was the first Antarctic manned flight.

The ship sailed along to the southwest corner of the Ross Sea and the crew erected their prefabricated hut on a spur protruding into what Ross had named McMurdo Sound. The spur became known as Hut Point. Much science was accomplished on the expedition, a route was pioneered up the Ferrar Glacier and one sledging party got within 532 miles of the Pole. The grail was surely within human grasp. The ship then became so firmly stuck in the ice that the men were obliged to spend a second winter in the south. Two relief vessels came down from England, the *Morning* and the *Terra Nova*, with orders from the Admiralty to abandon the *Discovery* if necessary, but the beleaguered ship eventually freed itself on 16 February 1904.

Back at home, Scott tried to settle to an ordinary naval career, but he became restless for the south. Antarctica offered him the opportunity to rise above his peers. By enduring the hardship of the south he, like so many others before and after, could distinguish himself in the eyes of the world. He referred to Antarctica in his diary as 'the promised land'.

In 1908 he married **Kathleen Bruce**. She was not the stereotypical explorer's wife, the little woman who stayed dutifully at home, giving birth and knitting. She was a sculptress with an independent spirit and a bohemian lifestyle. When they got engaged, Kathleen wrote to her brother, 'Man child woolly bird I've gone and been and done it now—I've gone and been and decided to marry Capt South Pole Scott...my trousseau won't take long cos there ain't agoin' to be no trousseau.'

Seven years after returning from his first trip, Scott was off once more, this time in the spartan converted whaler *Terra Nova*. Again science was the justification for the trip, but in his heart what Scott wanted was to reach the Pole. He knew the Norwegian expedition led by Amundsen was also in Antarctica and that a party was heading for the Pole, and it caused him a good deal of anxiety. The British team had again taken a prefabricated hut south, and this time erected it at Cape Evans on Ross Island, in the lee of Mount Erebus and about twelve miles north of Hut Point where they had been based last time. A happy winter was spent in the hut, with much talk of the Norwegians. In the total darkness of the long polar night **Edward 'Bill' Wilson** pulled a sledge from Cape Evans to Cape Crozier with **'Birdie' Bowers**, a tough little navy officer called Birdie because he had a beak nose, and **Apsley Cherry-Garrard**, the youngest member of the expedition, in order to collect emperor penguin eggs. No human being had yet examined such eggs. This epic journey took five weeks, the Fahrenheit temperature dropped to eighty below (−45°C), the tent blew away, their necks were frozen into the same position for hours and when they finally got back to the hut the others had to use tin openers to get their clothes off. In *The Worst Journey in the World*, a book which deals with the whole expedition, though the title refers to the march to Crozier, Cherry-Garrard artlessly turns the journey into the quest for truth and the penguin eggs into a symbol of its spiritual goal.

Scott and his party set out on 24 October 1911 using two dog teams, ten of the 19 Manchurian ponies which had endured the voyage to Antarctica and two motor sledges (one of the three sledges brought south had already gone through the ice). The ponies were in the charge of **Lawrence 'Titus' Oates**, a captain in the Sixth Inniskilling Dragoons and the only army man on the trip. He, unfortunately, had not chosen them, and although he slaved to keep them alive he knew that they had little chance—they were a feeble lot from the start. The surviving ponies were shot as planned when the polar party had crossed the Ross Ice Shelf.

Scott had chosen the Beardmore Glacier as his route up over the coastal mountains on to the polar plateau. He did not take dogs up, as it was, he judged, too gruelling, and there was not enough food, so he sent them back with a support party. The British explorers had muddled opinions upholding the moral virtues of dogless travel.

Eight men slogged up the glacier contending with crevasses, crucifying winds and low temperatures. The plan was that four men would continue to the Pole and four turn back. Scott had not yet made his final selection, but the food and fuel was already divided into four-man portions. Yet here Scott made a controversial decision. He announced that five men were to make the dash for the Pole: himself, Wilson, Oates, Bowers and Petty Officer 'Taff' Evans, a huge, genial Welshman. On 5 January 1912 the three others turned back 168 miles from the Pole.

The five men went on. Bowers had no skis. They had problems, but they also had hope. 'What castles one builds,' Scott wrote in his journal, 'now that the Pole is ours!' But there were to be no castles. On 16 January 1912 they saw a black flag flapping on the hard white ice at ninety degrees south. The Norwegians had beaten them to it. Scott wrote, 'The worst has happened.' The next day, when they got there, he wrote, 'Great God! This is an awful place and terrible enough for us to have laboured to it without the reward of priority.' They had reached the South Pole a month after Amundsen, and found the remains of his camp. The five of them put up their own tent, took observations, unpacked the camera and photographed themselves as they had been instructed by Herbert Ponting, the expedition photographer. Wilson made some sketches.

Their hearts, though, were broken. The 900-mile return journey looked desperate, now there was no promise of reward. They were tragically unlucky with the weather. Evans died during the march home, at the base of Beardmore. He had been the first to weaken, perhaps because he was so enormous. It was said that he died of concussion after a fall, but in truth the cause of his death has never been established. Titus Oates had badly frost-bitten feet and shortly after Evans died he made his famous sacrifice, walking to his death from the tent with the words, 'I am going outside. I may be some time.' Scott and his two remaining companions, Wilson and Bowers, perished in their tent, holed up in a blizzard eleven miles from a supply depot.

The tent was found by a search party from the Cape Evans hut the following spring. The rest of the men had endured a long winter of ebbing hope, knowing that their five colleagues must have perished. On the sledge outside the tent they found thirty-five pounds of rocks. To the end Scott had clung to science, as if that justified it all.

Knowing that he was about to die, and assessing that there was a good chance that the tent would be found by members of his party the following spring, Scott wrote a batch of final letters, and these were indeed found, along with his diary. Scott was a good writer, and his words scorched themselves into the national consciousness. 'We are weak, writing is difficult', said his Message to the Public, 'but for my own sake I do not regret this journey, which has shown that Englishmen can endure hardships, help one another, and meet death with as great a fortitude as ever... Had we lived I should have had a tale to tell of the hardihood, endurance, and courage of my companions which would have stirred the heart of every Englishman. These rough notes and our dead bodies must tell the tale...'

When Kathleen learnt he had died, she said she regretted nothing but his suffering. His courageous last notes were a source of great inspiration to her, and she brought up their son Peter (who became a distinguished naturalist) to be immensely proud of his father.

Scott wrote this last words in 1912, and it was 1913 before the message got home. Very soon England was going to need all the heroic role models it could muster. Nothing was ever quite the same after the Armageddon of Flanders and Ypres, and Scott became a symbol of the demise of the old-fashioned Englishman. This is what Apsley Cherry-Garrard wrote in *The Worst Journey in the World*:

> *Superficially they failed. I have heard discussions of their failure. The same men would have discussed the failure of Christ hanging upon the cross: or of Joan of Arc burning at the stake... To me, and perhaps to you, the interest of this story is the men, and it is the spirit of the men, 'the response of the spirit', which is interesting, rather than what they did or failed to do: except in a superficial sense they never failed. That is how I see it, and I knew them pretty well. It is a story about human minds with all kinds of ideas and questions involved, which stretch beyond the furthest horizons.*

'The Boss'—Sir Ernest Shackleton

Ernest Shackleton was in the merchant navy—a very different beast from its Royal equivalent. He first went south aboard *Discovery*, under Scott's command. On that expedition he sledged to the 81st parallel with Scott and Wilson, but was eventually invalided home with scurvy. We can only speculate as to how much that 'failure' cost him, emotionally. In 1907 Shackleton set out aboard *Nimrod* as leader, at last, of his own expedition, and on that journey, on which he took Manchurian ponies, he got to within 97 nautical miles of the Pole. It was, at the time, the furthest south ever reached. On the *Nimrod* expedition scientists **Douglas Mawson**, **Alastair Mackay** and the 50-year-old **T.W. Edgeworth David** reached the South Magnetic Pole—the first men to achieve that goal. The same three summited Erebus in the summer of 1908. Members of the expedition discovered the Beardmore Glacier, which they named after the industrialist who had supported them.

In 1914 Shackleton went south again, leading the ambitious Imperial Transantarctic Expedition on which two ships, the *Endurance* and the *Aurora*, deposited parties of men on opposite sides of the continent. The plan was that one party, led by Shackleton, was to sledge across Antarctica while the other laid depots on the opposite side. But *Endurance* was crushed by pack ice in the Weddell Sea, and zigzagged for hundred of miles in the pincers of an ice floe before finally succumbing on 27 October 1915.

At first the 28 men tried to manhaul the few supplies they had saved over the ice to Snow Hill Island 312 miles away or Paulet Island a little further, but the huge ice ridges meant that it was an almost impossible task, as they only covered about a mile a day, and exhausted themselves in the process. So they camped on an ice floe and stayed there until April 1916, when they launched the three lifeboats from the *Endurance*. For a week they battled to reach Elephant Island. When they got there, exhausted beyond the power of speech, Shackleton had not slept for 100 hours. There was no hope of a chance rescue, so Shackleton had to make a plan. He decided to set out for South Georgia 800 miles away in the *James Caird*, a 22ft lifeboat already battered from its journey from the place where the *Endurance* had sunk. They patched it up as best they could with parts from the other two boats, finished off the seams with seal blood and artist's paints, and five men set out on the most incredible journey in the annals of Antarctic exploration.

What they endured beggars belief. They were soaking wet all the time, their mouths and tongues were so swollen through thirst that they could barely swallow, and two of the sleeping bags were so irredeemably sodden that they tossed them overboard. After 15 days, approaching South Georgia, they were driven so close to land that they had to crane their necks to look up at the top of the crag. Frank Worsley, skipper of the *Caird*, said later that for three hours they looked death square in the eye, and that he felt annoyed that nobody would ever know they had got so far.

On the 17th day after leaving Elephant Island, on 10 May 1916, the *James Caird* reached King Haakon Bay on the uninhabited west coast of South Georgia. The three of them who were able—the Boss, as Shackleton was known, Thomas Crean and Frank Worsley—

struggled over hitherto unclimbed mountains in the middle of South Georgia and reached the whaling station at Stromness Bay. What they looked like, we can only imagine. The manager of the whaling station knew Shackleton well, but when he saw him he said, 'Who are you?'

Once the Boss had revealed himself, his first question was, 'When was the war over?' (The war, of course, had half its course yet to run—and the killings already numbered millions.)

The three exhausted men lying on the other side of South Georgia were duly retrieved, and after three rescue attempts Shackleton got to Elephant Island in a Chilean ship called *Yelcho* and found that the 22 men he had left there had all survived. When he was rowed ashore in a lifeboat he threw a packet of tobacco ahead of him. He knew his men pretty well.

It was an exceptionally difficult ice year, and on the other side of the continent the ten men of the Ross Sea Party also got into severe difficulties. They had laid supply depots to the base of the Beardmore Glacier by manhauling upwards of 1500 miles despite the fact that their ship, the *Aurora*, had blown out to sea before they had unloaded all their stores. They had to make trousers out of canvas tents left in the Cape Evans hut by Scott, and some of the men did not wash or change their clothes for two years. They were led by one-eyed **Aeneas Mackintosh**, and slogged on despite the fact that Shackleton and the other five who were supposed to be marching across from the opposite coast never came. How could they have known? Later, Mackintosh fell sick, and another man, **Ernest Joyce**, took over the leadership by default. On the first page of his book, *The South Polar Trail*, Joyce says that the hardships 'were almost beyond human endurance'. 'If there is a hell,' he wrote, 'this is the place, and the sleeping bags are worse than hell.'

The padre who had gone with them, **Spencer-Smith**, had got scurvy and died after weeks lashed to the sledge, often unconscious. Then, when they had laid the depots and got back to Hut Point, Mackintosh, who had recovered, and **V.G. Hayward**, who was in charge of the dogs, their minds fogged by suffering, set out across the fragile ice for the other hut at Cape Evans. They were never seen again. It has been said that Shackleton made a rare error of judgement in choosing Mackintosh. He might have done so out of loyalty, because Mackintosh had lost his eye on Shackleton's previous expedition, aboard *Nimrod*.

Twenty-five months after they had left civilisation, Shackleton came in the *Aurora* to fetch the survivors of the Ross Sea Party. In his 90th year, back in Australia, one of the men, Dick Richards, said that he had never recovered from the experience. But he also said that he didn't regret what they had done, despite the fact that in material terms it was futile. 'It was something that the human spirit accomplished,' he said.

After the First World War, Shackleton left Britain again, this time aboard *Quest*, with the aim of mapping an unknown sector of Antarctic coastline. Antarctica had a power over him, and the way he expressed it helps explain the motivation of many men who have repeatedly been drawn to the south. 'The stark polar lands', he wrote, 'grip the hearts of the men who have lived on them in a manner that can hardly be understood by the people who have never got outside the pale of civilisation.' On the journey out on the

Quest, the Boss died. He was buried in South Georgia and his second-in-command, **Frank Wild**, took over the leadership and carried out scientific investigations in Antarctica before returning home.

Shackleton was slightly larger than lifesize. His qualities of leadership were unsurpassed, and he earned the respect, love and devotion of all his men. He cherished a romantic vision of the world, and enjoyed writing as well as reading poetry. He was also a very human figure. Despite having a wife and family, he enjoyed the company of other women, and according to his doctors he smoked and drank too much. More than any other figure in polar history, Shackleton is the role model chosen by modern explorers.

Roald Amundsen

Norway had recently separated from Sweden, and Roald Amundsen put his young country on the map. He had extensive experience in the north, made the first transit in one vessel of the Northwest Passage, and knew **Fridtjof Nansen**, the greatest polar explorer of all (though he never went south). It was Nansen perhaps who best summed up the mysterious force that drives men to explore. He said it was 'the power of the unknown over the human spirit'.

Amundsen was planning to reach the North Pole, but when he heard that **Frederick Cook** claimed to have got there, he decided to go south, and set out in 1910 aboard *Fram*—though he didn't tell the crew or the rest of the world his true destination until he reached Madeira, off the north African coast. Until then, only his brother knew. It was an extraordinary decision, and casts light on Amundsen's motivation. He wanted to achieve something great in the world. Above all, he wanted to be remembered as a man who took risks and succeeded at the hardest thing. He was single-minded, which perhaps explains why he never married. The peace of the polar regions never left him any peace at home. In his book about the journey to the Pole, he said that when he and his men left Antarctica they knew that, 'When everyday life came with its cares and worries, it might well happen that we should look back with regret to our peaceful and untroubled existence at [their Antarctic base] Framheim.'

Amundsen took 97 dogs trained in Greenland, and landed in Antarctica ten days before Scott. *Fram* had been designed so it could drift safely with the ice in the Arctic. He made his base actually on the ice shelf, 400 miles east of where Scott erected his hut at Cape Evans on Ross Island. The team began a vigorous sledging programme, and laid depots over the icefields in preparation for the assault on the Pole. They weren't interested in science. Amundsen wanted to be the first man to reach 90°S, and admitted it.

In the course of those early explorings, Amundsen named Mount Betty after his housekeeper who had knitted vests for them all. He started for the Pole in September and was turned back by bad weather. In his eagerness he had set off too early. It was an uncharacteristic mistake. The polar party left Framheim for the second time on 19 October 1911 with four sledges and 48 dogs. They went up the Axel Heiberg Glacier (which they named) and started killing their dogs for food. **Helmer Hanssen**, **Oscar Wisting**, **Sverre**

Hassel, Olav Bjaaland and Amundsen reached 90°S on 14 December 1911 and raised a Norwegian flag on the iron-hard ice at the South Pole. They made a camp, which they called Polheim, and conducted a wide sweep of the area to make sure they didn't miss the Pole itself. When they set off for home, Amundsen left a message in a tent for Scott, asking him to forward a letter to King Haakon in the event of the Norwegian party being lost on the return journey. This must have been a bitter pill for Scott.

This return trip, according to Amundsen's account, was as gruelling as a country bike-ride followed by a picnic in a poppyfield. The depots they had laid were so plentiful that it was as if they were in 'the fleshpots of Egypt'. On 25 January 1912 they arrived back at Framheim. Everyone was asleep, so the polar party mustered outside the hut and went in together. 'Is it you?' replied the first sleepyhead. In five days the *Fram* was heading home. Why linger? Amundsen reasoned. His mission had been accomplished.

Douglas Mawson

Mawson was born in Shipley, West Yorkshire, but his parents emigrated to Australia when he was two. He went south four times, first on Shackleton's *Nimrod* and subsequently as leader of his own expeditions. Mawson was different from Amundsen, Scott and Shackleton, because he was a scientist—a geologist, to be precise. He had more detailed knowledge of his field of endeavour, and less elevated ideas about what he wanted to achieve, than the other men leading expeditions south at that time.

In 1911 Mawson led the Australasian Antarctic Expedition aboard *Aurora*. This was the first expedition to take a plane to the ice. It didn't have wings, but it was indubitably a plane. It was a Vickers open-cockpit job which had crashed on its test flight in Australia, but Mawson took it anyway as an 'air-tractor sledge', to pull loads. On the Far Eastern Sledging Journey across George V Land in 1912–13 Mawson made the most legendary one-man journey in the history of Antarctic exploration. He began travelling with two companions, **Xavier Mertz** and **B.E.S. Ninnis**. First he watched Ninnis disappear down a crevasse with almost all the food. Then he had to deal with Mertz going mad from food poisoning and biting off his own finger. (Only after Ninnis has disappeared down the crevasse does Mawson refer to Mertz by his Christian name in his diary.) There was no hope of rescue, so Mawson had to struggle on for hundreds of miles, heading back to his Commonwealth Bay base. His chances looked hopeless. He ate the dogs, eyes and all, and noted on 11 January that his own body was rotting through lack of nourishment. Rumours of cannibalism still surface in Australia from time to time. When he eventually crested the hill behind the base, he saw the ship sailing away. A few men had stayed behind, however, in case their lost leader and his two companions showed up after all. When he staggered up to the hut, Mawson was almost half his normal weight. The first person who saw him was a member of the expedition who knew Mawson very well. This man screwed up his face, peered at the wreck in front of him and said, 'Which one are you?'

This led to another epic when Captain Davis took the *Aurora* back to pick up Mawson and his team and didn't leave the bridge for seven days and seven nights.

Sixteen years later, Mawson was back. How had he been able to forget the bad times? In his diary he wrote about the peace of the south, and it was this that he remembered, not the frostbite. 'At times', he recorded, 'during the long hours of steady tramping across the trackless snowfields, one's thoughts flow on a clear and limpid stream, and the mind is unruffled and composed...' On the second expedition he led a 40-man joint British, Australian and New Zealand expedition with the intention of charting the 2500 miles of coastline between Kaiser Wilhelm II Land and Coats Land.

Mawson ended his career as Professor of Geology and Mineralogy at Adelaide University. He was a man of action, little given to introspection and with none of Shackleton's romanticism and poetic flair. Frank Hurley, the photographer who went south with both Mawson and Shackleton, summed up the difference between the two men like this. 'Shackleton grafted science on to exploration—Mawson added exploring to science.' But the continent gripped Mawson's imagination. He wrote later of Antarctica, 'We came to probe its mystery, to reduce this land in terms of science, but there is always the indefinable which holds aloof yet which rivets our souls.'

Unsung Heroes

The stories of the Big Four—Scott, Shackleton, Amundsen and Mawson—have often been told. But there are many unsung heroes. **Thomas Crean** was an Irish seaman in the Royal Navy and a last-minute addition to Scott's 1901 *Discovery* expedition. In 1911 he went south with Scott again, and on one occasion made a heroic rescue by leaping among the ice floes. On the polar journey he sledged to the most southerly depot on the polar plateau as a member of the last support party, then on the return trek to the Cape Evans hut Crean and fellow seaman **William Lashly** pulled the sickening Lieutenant (later Admiral and Sir) **Teddy Evans**. Eventually Evans became too ill even to be pulled, so Lashly stayed with him in the tent and Crean set off for help. When help arrived, a dog entered the tent and Evans wrote in his diary that he 'gave the hairy old Siberian face the kiss that was meant for Lashly'.

Then, in 1914, Shackleton took Crean on the ill-fated *Endurance*. Crean made the journey in the *James Caird* to South Georgia and was one of the three on the march over the mountains. Is there any man in history who has more experience of polar travel the hard way than Thomas Crean? He was an earthy man, entirely without guile. When he left Elephant Island, Frank Worsley, who was with him, described in his diary the farewell speeches of the men they were leaving behind. 'As for Crean, they said things that ought to have made him blush, but what would make Crean blush would make a butcher's dog drop its bone.' When it was all over, Crean went back to County Kerry in Ireland and founded the South Pole Inn in Annascaul, which still exists. Teddy Evans dedicated his bestselling book *South with Scott* to Crean and Lashly.

Victor Campbell is another unknown figure whose Antarctic feats of survival deserve to be remembered. He was stranded on Inexpressible Island for eight months with five men in their summer clothes and two months' rations during the Antarctic winter of 1912.

Campbell was an Old Etonian, a scientist and first officer on the *Terra Nova* on Scott's second expedition. He went to Antarctica partly because his marriage was rocky. Having been conveyed to the edge of the Ross Ice Shelf by the *Terra Nova* in January 1911, the intention of the Eastern Party, which consisted of Campbell, three seamen and two officers, was to carry out extensive surveying work, but they failed to find an eastern landing. Initiative being the key to Antarctic science then as now, they went north to Cape Adare instead.

On the way, much to the surprise of both groups, they met Amundsen and the other Norwegians in the Bay of Whales. When the watchman of the *Fram* saw the *Terra Nova* sailing past, he brought out his gun, which he loaded with six bullets, and an English phrasebook from which he quickly learnt to say 'Hello, how are you this morning?' The encounter was cordial, and they inspected each other's quarters. The British were astonished at the efficiency with which the Norwegians handled their dogs, and Amundsen recorded in his diary that after the visitors left all the Norwegians caught colds.

At Cape Adare (where Borchegrevink had landed), Campbell and his five men waved the ship goodbye and became the Northern Party. After a fruitful season the *Terra Nova* picked them up again and dropped them at what became Inexpressible Island, supposedly for six weeks. But when it came to fetch them that time, it failed to get through the pack ice and had to return to New Zealand, leaving Campbell and his men marooned in an ice-hole for eight months.

The men got used to a meat and fat diet, though its high acid content meant that some frequently wet themselves. They suffered from a painful condition they called 'igloo back', their lives so troglodytic and their faces so caked with blubber that they were recognisable only by their voices. After eight months on the edge of endurance they had to trek 230 miles back to the Cape Evans hut on Ross Island, and when they got there, they learnt that Scott and the others had perished.

It was the escape from the nine-to-five that appealed to these men and impelled them to go south. When the young scientist Raymond Priestley was apprehended in the Cambridge University library one day and asked, 'How would you like to go to the Antarctic, Ray?' he replied immediately, 'I'd go anywhere to get out of this damned place.' He became one of Scott's men. Once they got there, Antarctica vindicated their hopes. 'There, if anywhere', wrote the scientist Griffith Taylor, Priestley's contemporary, 'is life worthwhile.' On the whole there is very little complaint in their diaries. If they did moan, it was about each other, not Antarctica.

Japanese and German Expeditions

In 1910 Lieutenant Nobu Shirase led a Japanese Antarctic Expedition in the *Kainan-Maru* (Southern Pioneer). It wasn't very successful, but, undaunted, Shirase returned the following year and met the Norwegian ship *Fram* in the Bay of Whales (*Fram* obviously enjoyed a number of visitors). Members of the two crews took tea together. Shirase led a mission he called a Dash Patrol over the Ross Ice Shelf and sledged beyond 80°S. Around the same time **William Filchner** led a German expedition of 35 men. They left Hamburg in the *Deutschland* in 1911 and sailed to the Weddell Sea.

The British Graham Land Expedition

The Antarctic Peninsula (known then as Graham Land) had been annexed in 1908 as part of the Falkland Islands Dependency. In 1934, **John Rymill** led the British Graham Land Expedition. Rymill's was a private venture, and it was chronically short of cash—the crew were obliged to straighten out packing-cases to retrieve nails. They had £3000 to buy a ship, and ended up with the *Penola*, a three-masted Brittany fishing schooner which they were able to equip with a De Havilland Fox Moth plane. She was away from 1934 until 1937.

They were dogged by bad luck at the beginning but went on to make numerous discoveries and survey great tracts of unknown territory. Most important of all, they discovered that Graham Land was the Antarctic Peninsula (it had been thought that it was part of an archipelago), much as Columbus must have declared that there was land west of Iberia. The expedition never got the recognition it deserved, though it achieved more knowledge per pound spent than any other expedition. **Duncan Carse**, a member, said, 'We were the expedition that links the Heroic Age—Scott, Shackleton, Amundsen and Mawson—with BAS of today. We lived and worked on the watershed between too little regard for personal welfare and too great a reliance on impersonal technology. We were the fortunate ones who practised Antarctic exploration at its all-time best.'

Origins of the British Antarctic Survey

Meanwhile from 1925 to 1939 the Falkland Islands Dependencies Government sponsored a series of investigations based at South Georgia. Called the Discovery Investigations and paid for with taxes from whale oil, one of the voyages included the first winter circumnavigation of the continent. Then, in 1943, the British Admiralty mounted a wartime expedition to the Antarctic Peninsula on behalf of the Colonial Office. It was named Operation Tabarin after a Parisian nightclub, and its purpose was both to detect enemy activities in Antarctic waters and to strengthen British claims to sovereignty of the Falkland Islands Dependencies (*see* **Geopolitics**, p.108). A party established a base on Deception Island, the southernmost of the South Shetlands, within some of the old whaling station buildings. Another base was established at Port Lockroy on Weincke Island a little further south. On 24 April 1944 the existence of Operation Tabarin was made public. Personnel continued to chart the peninsula and its islands until most of them returned home in 1946. Tabarin transmogrified into a civilian operation called the Falkland Islands Dependencies Survey, and in 1962 this became the British Antarctic Survey.

Still, it was the freedom from the nine-to-five that drew the men south, just as it had been for the previous generation. It was like reverting to childhood. **Kevin Walton** was in the Antarctic in 1946–8 on the peacetime British operation that was previously Tabarin. In his book *Two Years in the Antarctic* he wrote that life on base involved, 'the most riotous schoolboy rough and tumble that I'd known since the days before the war.'

The Age of Aviation

Not counting the balloons which flew with men aboard in 1902 on both Scott and Erich von Drygalski's expeditions, the first full-scale flight was made in 1928 when the Australian **Hubert Wilkins** flew for 11 hours along 1300 miles of the peninsula in a Lockheed monoplane. Wilkins, who had previously competed with American pilots in the Arctic, ran a small team funded by the Hearst newspaper empire. He wanted the honour of making the first Antarctic flight, and had no scientific objectives.

The newspapers saw it as a race between Wilkins and the American **Richard Byrd**, just as Scott and Amundsen had raced 17 years earlier. Hearst had allegedly offered Wilkins a huge sum of money if he beat Byrd to the Pole. On 20 December 1928, Byrd heard over the radio that he had indeed been beaten, though not to the Pole. Wilkins had flown the first plane in Antarctica, and he had done it down the peninsula. He reported mistakenly that it was not a peninsula but an island.

The next year Wilkins went back to his base planning to fly over the territory east of Little America (*see* below), and he said he would drop in on Byrd for Christmas dinner. Again, he was bankrolled by Hearst. Everyone was extremely jumpy about who was to be the first to the Pole, but Wilkins eventually cancelled his proposed flight, apparently because he couldn't find a stretch of flat sea ice for take-off.

Lincoln Ellsworth is perhaps the most famous exponent of early ice flying. In 1934, with Hubert Wilkins, he sailed to the American base Little America on the Ross Ice Shelf, planning to fly across the continent. The ice on which they had parked their plane split, however, so that was the end of another project. The next year Ellsworth tried to fly to Little America from the peninsula, but bad weather stopped him. Finally, in November 1935, together with the pilot **Herbert Hollick-Kenyon**, he made this last flight.

The depths to which territorial greed and overweening pride can afflict mere mortals had yet to reach its apogee in Antarctica. Just before the Second World War, in March 1939, Hitler decided that Antarctica too was to be part of the great Nazi Empire. He ordered several thousand steel-barbed swastikas, loaded them on to planes, put the planes on a ship called the *Schwabenland* and sent the whole lot south, telling the pilots, who had been out practising in the Alps, to drop their load over vast tracts of the icefields at 16-mile intervals. It has subsequently been suggested that the pilots simply dumped their load in one spot, on the basis that neither Hitler nor anybody else would ever know—but this, of course, is unknowable.

Richard Byrd flew over the Pole in 1947, on his second attempt. He said it was like flying in a bowl of milk. Byrd was a towering figure in the short history of Americans in Antarctica, though not a popular one, and several of his claims—such as his 1929 'flight over the South Pole' are regarded with suspicion. He made five journeys to the ice. The first was in 1928, when he established a base called Little America on the Bay of Whales, near the site of Amundsen's Framheim. This expedition took four aircraft equipped with skis, as well as 100 dogs.

Byrd's second expedition, only twenty-two years after Scott, was the most spectacular. On it he made the extraordinary decision to spend four and a half months alone at Bolling Advance Weather Station in the winter beginning March 1934. He was much criticised for this back at home, as he was leaving his team leaderless and possibly risking the lives of a rescue party. In truth there was no hope of rescue before the light returned. Byrd was slowly poisoned by carbon monoxide leaking from a defective stove, and the ordeal became a struggle for sanity. He survived until rescued, and his book *Alone* is one of the classics of polar exploration, whatever you think of him.

As for setting foot at the Pole, after Scott and his party departed in January 1912 nobody was there until 31 October 1956 when **Admiral George Dufek** stepped out of an R-4D plane called *Que será será*. The following month Americans began parachuting in materials, and construction of the first South Pole station began.

First Crossing

The Antarctic continent was crossed for the first time during the 1955–8 Commonwealth Transantarctic Expedition, which **Sir Vivien Fuchs** led with **Sir Edmund Hillary** in command of the New Zealand support party. Fuchs had already spent many seasons in the Antarctic, and in 1950 the Falkland Islands Dependencies Scientific Bureau was founded under his direction. As for Ed Hillary—he and Sherpa Tensing had been the first men to summit Everest. The Transantarctic expedition crossed 2150 miles of Antarctica from the Weddell Sea to the Ross Sea in 99 days, using dogs and tractors. Hillary was the first to travel overland to the Pole since Scott, and the first ever with vehicles—three farm tractors fitted with rubber treads, to be exact. At the Pole he was joined by Fuchs, who had travelled from the other side. In spite of the tractors, and in spite of the radio telephone and the electric sewing machine, the expedition seemed to mark the end of an unbroken line which Scott had started. Certainly, Antarctic exploration was never going to be the same again.

The First Women

Observant readers will have noticed that this history is exclusively male. The Norwegian **Caroline Mikkelsen** became the first woman to set foot on the continent on 20 February 1935. Eleven years later the American pilot Harry Darlington took his wife **Jennie** south when he was third-in-command of **Finn Ronne**'s expedition to Stonington Island. Ronne's wife also went. The experiment was not deemed a success—but it wasn't the women's fault (they got the blame, of course). The whole expedition was a disaster, though the Ronne Ice Shelf was added to the maps. Jennie wrote in her book *My Antarctic Honeymoon*, 'It has been like living in a male locker room.'

Once the various official government programmes were up and running in Antarctica, women were slowly introduced—so slowly that they might have been a potentially deadly bacterium which the men were worried might infect them in the south, lacking in resistance as they undoubtedly were. The Soviets brought the first female non-wife south in 1957, and two years later the Australian programme followed suit. One of the first Australian women selected wrote later, 'We were invaders in a man's realm and we were regarded with suspicion.' The Americans sent the first four women south as programme participants in 1969, inciting the memorable headline, 'Powder Puff Explorers Invade the South Pole'.

The first child born in the vicinity of the continent was supposedly to a waitress aboard a Russian whaler in 1948. The Argentinians began bringing spouses south to their bases on the peninsula in 1977 in order to reinforce their territorial claim, and in 1978 one of them obligingly gave birth—though she was flown south seven months pregnant. By 1984 the Chileans were at it too, and they even established a school.

What's Left?

During the 1960s, satellite photographs joined up the last remaining dots on the map. By the time man took his first tentative steps on the moon—but only then—the white continent had yielded its last secrets. Or had it?

There are few Antarctic 'firsts' left now. Still, enterprising men and women who have something to prove to themselves and the world are still strapping on skis and trying to cross this bit for the first time in such and such a way, or that bit for the first time in another way. The second land crossing took place in 67 days in the 1980–1 season when **Sir Ranulph Fiennes**, **Charlie Burton** and **Oliver Shepard** drove small sledge-pulling snowmobiles. It constituted one leg of the ambitious three-year English Transglobe expedition which took in both poles. Nine years later the American **Will Steger** led the International Trans-Antarctica Expedition and made the third crossing of the continent. Six men travelled by ski, their sledges hauled by 36 specially bred huskies, and they became the first to cross the continent on foot. Steger's companions were from five different countries: Russia, Japan, the UK, China and France. They took the longest route (from near the tip of the peninsula to the Russian base Mirny on the east coast, via the Pole), covering a colossal 3741 miles in 220 days.

During the same period the Austrian **Reinhold Messner**, possibly the greatest mountaineer alive, and **Arved Fuchs** (no relation to Sir Vivien) manhauled sledges across Antarctica from the South American side to the New Zealand side via the Pole. Messner is a purist, although he and Fuchs were resupplied by aircraft on their trek. 'Whoever moves in the Antarctic with motor vehicles, helicopters and aircraft', he wrote in his book, *Antarctica: Both Heaven and Hell* 'is like a car tourist who squats in his capsule and feels nothing of his surroundings.' This is a typical male view. Messner's talk of the tranquillity of unencumbered travel and the purity of his vision of the continent is somewhat spoilt by the terrible quarrel he had with Fuchs, brought about, inevitably, by a surfeit of testos-

TOP RIGHT: *Captain Scott's hut at Cape Evans, in the lee of Mount Erebus.*

ABOVE AND FAR RIGHT: *Inside Scott's hut at Cape Evans.*

NEAR RIGHT: *Inside Shackleton's hut at Cape Royds.*

ABOVE: *Southern Party on board the* Nimrod.
L to R: Wild, Shackleton, Marshall and Adams.

BELOW: *Shackleton's* Endurance *is crushed
by pack ice, 1914–16.*

terone. 'I was as hurt as after a broken love affair,' wrote Messner unconvincingly. The whole business was well summed up by a business journalist in Germany: 'It is a tragedy: two men battle for months and thousands of kilometres across an uninhabited ice desert, survive the murderous cold and annihilating storms, in short, accomplish a performance such as no one before them has accomplished—and what sticks in the mind of most television viewers, newspaper and magazine readers? That the pair have quarrelled.'

On the subject of quarrels, in 1992–3 **Mike Stroud** and **Sir Ranulph Fiennes** attempted the first coast-to-coast crossing unsupported by men, animals or machines, although they were too weak to continue over the floating Ross Ice Shelf to open water to finish the crossing as they had intended, and were compelled to radio for a rescue plane. They pulled sledges which at the beginning weighed nearly 500 pounds each for 95 days and 1350 miles. When they got back, like most of the men whose competitive instincts have compelled them to test themselves to the limit on the ice, they bickered publicly about who had been in charge, or some such nonsense.

In the same season, four skiers on the American Women's Antarctic Expedition set out from Patriot Hills at 80°S and reached the Pole. There were no quarrels.

In December 1994 the first Japanese overland expedition arrived at the South Pole, also from Patriot Hills, and on Christmas Day that same year **Liv Arnesen** became the first Norwegian woman to ski in—she had pulled her own sledge for five weeks, from the Hercules Inlet on the Ronne Ice Shelf, which is about 550 miles from the coast. The following season **Roger Mear** made an aborted attempt at a solo crossing of the continent a decade after re-enacting Cherry-Garrard's Cape Crozier trek on the Footsteps of Scott expedition. In 1996–7 Ran Fiennes set out on a much-publicised solo, unsupported crossing, racing against men from several other nations, including a Norwegian, until he was forced by severe gallstones to be flown home. So it goes on. And it will go on, at least until the next ice age puts a stop to it. This is how Apsley Cherry-Garrard saw it in his book *The Worst Journey in the World*:

> *And I tell you, if you have the desire for knowledge and the power to give it physical expression, go out and explore. If you are a brave man you will do nothing: if you are fearful you may do much, for none but cowards have need to prove their bravery. Some will tell you that you are mad, and nearly all will say, "What is the use?" For we are a nation of shopkeepers, and no shopkeeper will look at research which does not promise him a financial return within a year. And so you will sledge nearly alone, but those with whom you sledge will not be shopkeepers: that is worth a good deal. If you march your Winter Journeys you will have your reward, so long as all you want is a penguin's egg.*

Landmark Chronology

1773–5	James Cook crosses Antarctic Circle and (1775) makes first landing on South Georgia.
1820	Fabien Bellingshausen makes first sighting of Antarctic continent (probably).
1821	Sealer John Davis becomes the first man to set foot on the Antarctic continent (probably).
1841	James Clark Ross penetrates pack ice to 78°S.
1898	*Belgica* expedition becomes the first to winter in the pack ice.
1899	Carsten Borchgrevink's expedition winters on the continent.
1901–4	Scott's *Discovery* expedition. Men sledge to 82°S.
1907–9	Shackleton's *Nimrod* expedition. A party sledges to within 97 nautical miles of the Pole.
1910–12	Roald Amundsen's expedition in the *Fram*. A team reaches the South Pole on 14 December 1911.
1910–13	Scott's *Terra Nova* expedition. Five men reach the South Pole five weeks after Amundsen, and all die on the return journey.
1911–14	Douglas Mawson's Australasian Antarctic Expedition to Terre Adélie.
1914–17	Shackleton's Transantarctic expedition and his epic journey to South Georgia after the *Endurance* is crushed.
1922	Shackleton dies at South Georgia during his third expedition.
1934–7	British Graham Land Expedition discovers that the Antarctic peninsula is not an archipelago.
1935	Caroline Mikkelsen becomes the first woman to set foot on the continent.
1947	Richard Byrd makes first flight over the South Pole.
1955–8	Continent crossed for the first time by Vivien Fuchs and Edmund Hillary's Commonwealth Transantarctic Expedition.
1956	George Dufek's plane lands at Pole—first man there since Scott.
1957–8	International Geophysical Year. Twelve countries establish 50 bases on Antarctica and sub-Antarctic islands.
1959	Antarctic treaty, applicable to all territory south of 60°S, signed by 12 nations.
1961	Antarctic Treaty comes into force.
1991	Protocol on Environmental Protection imposes a 50-year moratorium on extracting oil and mining minerals.

The following guidelines have been drawn up and adopted by the International Association of Antarctica Tour Operators. The object of this document was and is to protect the fragile Antarctic ecosystem and minimise visitor impact.

Do not disturb, harass or otherwise interfere with the wildlife

Most Antarctic species exhibit a lack of fear which allows you to approach relatively close; however, remember that the austral summer is a time for courting, mating, nesting, rearing young and moulting. If any animal changes or stops its activities upon your approach, you are too close! Disturbing nesting birds may cause them to expose their eggs or offspring to predators or cold. Be especially careful when taking photographs, since it is easy not to notice adverse reactions of animals when concentrating through the lens of a camera, and maintain a low profile, since animals can be intimidated by people standing over them. The disturbance of some animals, notably fur seals and nesting skuas, may elicit an aggressive, even dangerous, response.

- *Never touch the animals.*

- *Maintain a distance of at least 15ft from penguins, all nesting birds and true (crawling) seals, and 50ft from fur seals.*

- *Give animals the right of way.*

- *Do not position yourself between a marine animal and its path to the water, or between a parent and its young.*

- *Always be aware of your surroundings; stay outside the periphery of bird rookeries and seal colonies.*

- *Keep noise to a minimum.*

- *Do not feed the animals, either ashore or from the ship.*

Guidelines of Conduct for Visitors

Do not walk on or otherwise damage fragile plants (lichens, mosses and grasses)

Poor soil and harsh living conditions mean growth and regeneration of these plants is extremely slow. Most lichens, which grow only on rocks, hard-packed sand and gravel, and bones, are extremely fragile. Damage from human activity among moss beds can last decades.

Leave nothing behind, and take only memories and photographs

- *Leave no litter ashore, and remove any litter you may find while ashore. Dispose of all litter properly.*

- *Do not take souvenirs, including whale and seal bones, live or dead animals, rocks, fossils, plants, other organic material or anything which may be of historical or scientific value.*

Do not interfere with protected areas or scientific research

Areas of special scientific concern are clearly delineated by markers and/or described in official records. The expedition staff know these sites. Scientific research in Antarctica is in the interest of everyone—visitors, scientists and laymen.

- *Do not enter buildings at the research stations unless invited to do so.*

- *Avoid entering all officially protected areas and do not disturb any on-going scientific studies.*

Historic huts may only be entered when accompanied by a properly authorised escort

Historic huts are essentially museums, and they are all officially maintained and monitored by various governments.

- *Nothing may be removed from or disturbed within historic huts.*

Do not smoke during shore excursions

Great care must be taken to safeguard against this danger, particularly around wildlife areas, historic huts, research buildings and storage facilities.

Stay with your group or with one of the ship's leaders when ashore

- *Follow the directions of the expedition staff.*

- *Never wander off alone or out of sight of others.*

- *Do not hike on to glaciers or large snow fields, as there is a real danger of falling into hidden crevasses.*

For a full bibiography of books and journals about Antarctica, see *The Antarctic* (Clio Press, Oxford 1994) compiled by James Meadows, William Mills and Harry King. Be aware that many of the books in it, and certain ones listed below, are out of print: you'll have to borrow them from a library, or scour second-hand bookshops. Antarctic books do pop up frequently in second-hand or antiquarian bookshops, so it's worth keeping your eyes open.

General

Bainbridge, Beryl, *The Birthday Boys*, Duckworth, London 1991. Excellent novel about Captain Scott's last expedition.

Campbell, David, *The Crystal Desert*, Houghton Mifflin, New York 1992. Scientist's musings after three seasons around the peninsula. Very good.

Hooper, Meredith, *A is for Antarctica*, Piccolo Books, London 1991. Easy-to-read fact book for children which is also useful for adults.

Keneally, Thomas, *Victim of the Aurora*, William Collins, London & Sydney 1977. Mystery-thriller set in Antarctica.

Lopez, Barry, *Arctic Dreams*, Macmillan, New York 1986. Although it is about the wrong end of the earth, this is a wonderful treatise on polar regions in general. Available in paperback and well worth including in your luggage.

Mickleburgh, Edwin, *Beyond the Frozen Sea*, Bodley Head, London 1990. Personal and lyrical reflections on a place with a very special place in the author's heart.

Pyne, Stephen J., *The Ice*, University of Iowa Press, Iowa City 1986. A fat tour-de-force covering many aspects of the white continent. Not easy reading, but immensely worth a bit of effort.

Rowell, Galen, *Poles Apart*, Mountain Light Press, California 1995. Thought-provoking photographic book comparing north and south polar regions.

Spufford, Francis, *I May Be Some Time*, Faber & Faber, London, 1996. A fascinating treatise on the role of ice in the English imagination throughout history. For literary-minded readers.

Further Reading

Wheeler, Sara, *Terra Incognita: An Antarctic Journey*, Jonathan Cape, London 1996. Author's seven-month odyssey around Antarctica.

Various authors, *Antarctica: the Extraordinary History of Man's Conquest of the Frozen Continent*, Reader's Digest, Surrey Hills, Australia 1990 (second edition). All you ever needed to know, with masses of pictures.

Wildlife

Fothergill, Alastair, *Life in the Freezer*, BBC Books, London, 1993. Bestselling book of the BBC television series.

Harrison, Peter, *Seabirds: An Identification Guide*, Croom Helm, London 1983 (revised edition). Recommended by all the experts for ocean-going birdspotting.

Moss, Stanford and deLeiris, Lucia, *Natural History of the Antarctic Peninsula*, Columbia University Press, New York 1988. All the facts—and nicely illustrated with line drawings.

Parmalee, David Freeland, *Antarctic Birds*, University of Minnesota Press, Minneapolis 1992. Brilliant piece of kit for the committed spotter.

Soper, Tony, *Antarctica. A Guide to the Wildlife*, Bradt Publications, Chalfont St Peter 1994. User-friendly handbook with attractive illustrations.

History

Amundsen, Roald, *The South Pole*, John Murray, London 1912. Cheery account of the triumphant Norwegian expedition.

Baughmann, T.S., *Before the Heroes Came*, University of Nebraska Press, Lincoln, Nebraska 1994. Good book about the Antarctic explorers   of the 1890s.

Borchgrevink, C.E., *First on the Antarctic Continent*, George Newnes, London 1901. Memoirs of the man who led the first expedition to land on the continent, and also the first to winter.

Byrd, Richard E., *Discovery*, G.P. Putnam's Sons, New York 1935

Byrd, Richard E., *Alone*, G.P. Putnam's Sons, New York 1938. The grand old man of American Antarctic endeavours tells his own version of events.

Cherry-Garrard, Apsley, *The Worst Journey in the World*, Penguin Books, London 1922. The best polar book ever written. Cherry went south on Scott's second expedition, and this is his story.

Cook, F.A., *Through the First Antarctic Night*, William Heinemann, London 1900. Hard to get hold of, but a ripping yarn.

Dodge, Ernest S., *The Polar Rosses*, Faber & Faber, London 1973. Good, solid biography of James Clark Ross, one of the most important Antarctic explorers, and his uncle, famous for his explorarion in northern polar regions.

Dunnett, Harding McGregor, *Shackleton's Boat*, Neville & Harding, Cranbrook, Kent 1996. The story of the *James Caird*, with many illustrations.

Huntford, Roland, *Shackleton*, Hodder & Stoughton, London 1985

Huntford, Roland, *Scott and Amundsen*, Hodder & Stoughton, London 1979 (later republished as *The Last Place on Earth*). Both wonderful biographies, though the author's prejudice against Scott distorts the picture. The Scott and Amundsen book caused a furore when it was published as it debunks the heroic Scott myth.

Hurley, Frank, *Argonauts of the South*, G.P. Putnam's Sons, New York 1925. Shackleton's photographer tells his story.

Jacka, Frank & Eleanor (eds), *Mawson's Antarctic Diaries*, Adelaide University Press, Adelaide 1988. The great Australian Antarctican's records of his ground-breaking trips.

Lansing, Alfred, *Endurance*, Hodder & Stoughton, London 1959. The greatest Antarctic story ever told: how Shackleton pulled it off when the *Endurance* sank in 1915.

Lashly, William, *Under Scott's Command*, Victor Gollancz, London 1969. Lashly was one of the unsung heroes—he came from the lower decks—who went south with Scott.

Newman, Stanley (ed), *Shackleton's Lieutenant: The 'Nimrod' Diary of A.L.A. Mackintosh*, Polar Publications, Auckland 1990. Another ripping yarn.

Richards, R.W., *The Ross Sea Shore Party*, Scott Polar Research Institute, Cambridge 1962. These were the men laying the depots for Shackleton on the aborted 1914 Transantarctic expedition.

Rodgers, Eugene, *Beyond the Barrier*, Naval Institute Press, Annapolis 1990. Biography of Admiral Richard Byrd, the most controversial figure in American Antarctic history.

Ross, Sir James Clark, *A Voyage of Discovery and Research in the Southern and Antarctic Regions*, John Murray, London 1847. The great man's own story.

Rymill, John, *Southern Lights*, The Travel Book Club, London 1938. Rymill was the leader of the British Graham Land Expedition which made important discoveries around the peninsula in the thirties.

Scott, Captain Robert F., *The Voyage of the Discovery*, Macmillan, London 1905

Scott, Captain Robert F., *Scott's Last Expedition*, Smith, Elder & Co, London 1913. Both essential reading for anyone with an interest in history.

Shackleton, Ernest, *The Heart of the Antarctic*, William Heinemann, London 1909. A showman writes.

Shackleton, Ernest, *South*, William Heinemann, London 1919.

Thomson, David, *Scott's Men*, Allen Lane, London 1977. Controversial and scholarly analysis of Captain Scott and the dynamics of his expeditions. An enthralling read.

Wilson, Edward, *Diary of the 'Discovery' Expedition*, Humanities Press, New York 1967.

Wilson, Edward , *Diary of the 'Terra Nova' Expedition*, Blandford Press, London 1972. Wilson was Scott's right-hand man, a distinguished scientist and confidant to almost the entire crew. He died with Scott.

Young, Louisa, *A Great Task of Happiness*, Macmillan, London, 1995. Lively biography of Captain Scott's wife, Kathleen. She was not a typical explorer's spouse.

Modern Expeditions: Sailing

Klink, Amyr, *Between Two Poles*, Bloomsbury, London 1995. Poetic Brazilian single-handed yachtsman writes about his winter in Antarctica (and his journey to many other places).

Lewis, David, and George, Mimi, *Icebound in Antarctica*, Secker & Warburg, London 1987. Six-person expedition which wintered in Antarctica in a 65-foot yacht.

Ridgeway, John, Marie-Christine and Rebecca, *Then We Sailed Away*, Little, Brown, London 1996. Outdoorsy author sails to Antarctica with family in tow.

Modern Expeditions: Overland

Fiennes, Ranulph, *Mind over Matter*, Sinclair-Stevenson, London 1993. An account of the author's epic 1350 traverse with Mike Stroud (*see* below).

Mear, Roger and Swan, Robert, *In the Footsteps of Scott*, Jonathan Cape, London 1987. The story of an action-packed expedition to the Pole.

Messner, Reinhold, *Antarctica: Both Heaven and Hell*, Crowood Press, Marlborough 1991. The world's top mountaineer tells the story of his Antarctic expedition.

Steger, Will, and Bowermaster, John, *Crossing Antarctica*, Alfred A. Knopf, New York 1992. Six men and 36 dogs cross the continent on the 1989–90 International Trans-Antarctica Expedition.

Stroud, Mike, *Shadows on the Wasteland*, Jonathan Cape, London 1993. Story of the author's epic 1350-mile traverse with Ran Fiennes. Read straight after Fiennes' book, you wouldn't think the two men were on the same expedition.

Modern Expeditions: Climbing

Anderson, Robert Mads, *To Everest Via Antarctica*, Swan Hill Press, Shrewsbury 1996. Climbing solo on the highest peak on each of the world's seven continents.

Other Ports of Call

Bridges, E. Lucas, *The Uttermost Part of the Earth*, London 1948. If you are stopping in Tierra del Fuego you will find this book fascinating.

Headland, R., *The Island of South Georgia*, Cambridge University Press, Cambridge 1992. Authoritative and comprehensive.

Strange, Ian J., *The Falkland Islands and their Natural History*, David & Charles, Newton Abbot 1987. An excellent companion guide.

Strange, Ian J., *A Field Guide to the Wildlife of the Falkland Islands and South Georgia*, HarperCollins, London 1992. Straightforward and packed with information.

Index

Coats Land 125
cold-weather injuries 26–7, 29, 60, 82
Coleridge, Samuel Taylor 20, 96
Commonwealth Bay 53, 54, 132
Commonwealth Transantarctic Expedition 137
communications 80–81
condensation 29
Convention on the Conservation of Antarctic Marine Living Resources (CCAMLR) 115
Cook, Frederick A. 124
Cook, Captain James 44, 121–2
cormorants 98
Crean, Thomas 129, 133
Crozier, Cape 124
cruises 2–16, 25
   bargains 18
cruise ships 2, 5–14, 25, 26, 31, 32
currency see money

D-8 tractors 79
Darlington, Jennie 137
Dash-7 planes 79
David, T. W. Edgeworth 129
Davis, John 122
daylight/darkness 59, 82, 84
daytrips 16
Deception Island 25, 48, 135
dehydration 26, 77
demilitarisation 110, 111
desalination 74, 77
diamond dust 60
dinosaurs 70
'Discovery Hut' 54
diving 64, 70
   Falklands 42
   see also scuba-diving
doctors in Antarctica 82–3
dogs 78, 124, 127, 137
Dominican gulls 98
Drake Passage 48
Drake, Sir Francis 48, 120
drink 26, 77, 111
drysuits 64
Dry Valleys 54, 64–5, 84–5, 102, 117
Dufek, Admiral George 137
Dumont d'Urville, Jules 123
Dumont d'Urville Base 52, 53, 117
duty-free goods 31

East Antarctica 58
electronic mail 31, 80
Elephant Island 92, 129, 130
Ellsworth, Lincoln 136
Ellsworth Mountains 17, 58
email 31, 80
entry formalities 19
environment:
   awareness 25–6, 84–5, 103
   global pollution 66–7
   issues 65, 115–18
equipment see clothing
Erebus, Mount 55, 56, 104–5, 123, 129
Evans, Cape 53, 54, 55, 126–7, 130
Evans, Admiral Sir Edward (Teddy) 76, 133
Evans, 'Taff' 127–8
exploration see history

Falkland Islands 38–43, 39
   eating out 43
   history 40, 42–3
   information 40–1, 43
   sport 25, 40, 42
   travel 2–16, 40, 42
   where to stay 43
Falkland Islands Dependencies 44, 135, 137
Falklands War 42, 108
   see also Falkland Islands (history)
Faraday station 116
Fiennes, Sir Ranulph 81, 138, 139
Filchner, William 135
film 29
fire hazards 73–4
first aid 27, 82
fish 62–4, 99
fishing 63–4
   Falklands 42
flora see plant-life
food 26, 76–7
footwear 24, 73
fossils 69–70
France 108, 122, 125
frostbite 26, 60
frostnip 26
Fuchs, Arved 138
Fuchs, Sir Vivien 137
fur clothing 72
fur seals see seals

gear see clothing
Geographic South Pole 58–9
geography 58–9
geology 58–9, 62, 69–70
geopolitics 107–18
George V Land 14, 54, 132
Gerlache, Adrien de 124
Germany 100, 125, 135, 136
giant petrel 41
gifts:
   buying 30–31
   making 81
   taking 32
'glacier berries' 77
glacier glasses see sunglasses
glaciology 67–9
global warming 61, 68
gloves 25, 26, 29, 72–3
goggles 24, 27, 73
Gondwana 69
Goose Green (Falklands) 40
Graham Land see Antarctic Peninsula
Great Britain:
   and Antarctica 108, 113–14
   exploration history 120–24, 125–31, 133–6, 138–9
   see also British Antarctic Survey
Greater Antarctica 58, 69
Greeks 120
Greenpeace 115–16, 117
Grytviken 46, 100
gulls 95–6, 98

Half Moon Island 48
Halley Base 66, 79, 113–14
Hanson, Nikolai 51
Hanssen, Helmer 78, 131
hats 24, 73
Hayward, V. G. 130
headgear 24–5, 73
health 19, 26–7, 82–3
helicopters 79–80
Hercules planes 79
hiking 40, 42
Hillary, Sir Edmund 137
historic huts 48, 52–3, 54–5, 126–7, 142
history 108, 114–15, 119–40
   see also Falkland Islands; South Georgia
Hitler, Adolf 136
Hope Bay 48, 50

Hurley, Frank 133
huskies *see* dogs
huts 75, 111
    see also historic huts
hygiene 84–6
hypothermia 26

IAATO *see* International
    Association of Antarctica Tour
    Operators
ice 67–9
ice blink 60
icebreakers 63, 80
ice cores 68
ice shelves 58, 61
ice streams 68
igloos 75
Imperial Transantarctic Expedition
    see Shackleton, Sir Ernest
independent travel 18
India 110, 113
information 32
insects 88, 102
insurance 19
International Association of
    Antarctica Tour Operators
    (IAATO) 25–6
    guidelines 103, 141–2
International Geographical Year 110,
    114
International Polar Year Expedition
    44
International Trans-Antarctica
    Expedition 138
Islas Malvinas *see* Falkland Islands
isolation 83–4
Italy 111–12
    see also Terra Nova Bay

Jamesways 75
Japan 113, 134, 139
Joyce, Ernest 130

kelp gulls 98
Keppel Island 42
Kerguélen 59, 65
Kerguélen-Trémerac, Yves-Joseph
    de 122
King Edward Point 43, 46
King George Island 50, 82
    bank 28
    bases 7, 50, 82, 113
    Chile and 28, 82

shopping 30
    see also Teniente Rodolfo Marsh
krill 62–3, 99

lakes 64–5
Larsen, Captain C. A. 44, 100
Larsen Ice Shelf 61
Lashly, William 133
laundry 27, 86
lavatories 84–5
leisure 81–2
Lemaire Channel 50
Lesser Antarctica 58, 69
lichens 65, 101–2, 141
life sciences 62–5
Little America 136–7
London, Jack viii

McFarlane, John 123
Mackay, Alastair 129
Mackintosh, Aeneas 130
McMurdo, Archibald 124
McMurdo Sound 104, 124, 126
McMurdo Station *53*, 55, 56, 59,
    74, 118
    leisure 73, 74, 81–2
    shopping 30
Macquarie Island 11, 14, 65
Magellan, Ferdinand 93, 120
mail 27, 80, 110
mail-order 24, 31
Malvinas *see* Falkland Islands
maps 28, 41, 120
marine biology *see* biology
Mawson, Sir Douglas 76, 129,
    132–3
    Australasian Antarctic Expedition
    53, 54, 132
Mear, Roger 139
medical facilities 82–3
    see also health
medical research 70, 83
Melbourne, Mount 56
Melville, Herman, *Moby-Dick* 101
menstruation 85
Mertz, Xavier 132
Messner, Reinhold 138–9
meteorology *see* weather research
micro-organisms 102
Mikkelsen, Caroline 137
military personnel 110
mineral reserves 115

mines 41
mining 115–16
money 28, 30–31
    Falklands 41
mosses 65, 101–2, 141
Mounts: *see under given name*
museums 42, 46
    see also historic huts

Nansen, Fridtjof 78, 131
Nansen sledges 78
neck gaiters 73
New Zealand:
    and Antarctica 31, 63, 108, 112
    travel to 19
    see also Scott Base
Ninnis, B. E. S. 132
nitrates 65
Nordenskjöld, Otto 50, 124–5
North Pole 123, 124, 125
Norwegians 44, 108, 124, 131–2,
    134, 139
nuclear issues 110, 115

Oates, Lawrence 'Titus' 127–8
oil 39, 115
Operation Tabarin 135
ornithology *see* birds
ozone depletion 62, 66–7, 114

pack ice 68
Palmer, Nathaniel 122
Palmer Base *49*, 114
Paradise Harbour 50
parhelion 60
passports 19
Patriot Hills 17
Paulet Island 48, 50–51
Pebble Island 42, 43
pemmican 76
penguins 88–93, 103
    Adélie 50, 51, 53, 63, 89–90
    chinstrap 48, 50, 92–3
    emperor 63, 90–91
    Falklands 41
    gentoo 11, 51, 89, 91–2
    king 91
    macaroni 92
    Magellanic (jackass) 41, 93
    predators 96, 97
    research 63, 116, 127, 139
    rockhopper 92

Peru 113
petrels 41, 97
photography 28–30, 54–5
  see also wildlife
physics research 65–7
phytoplankton 62, 99
planes 79
plankton 64, 99
  see also phytoplankton
plant-life 65, 101–2, 103, 116, 141
  Falklands 39
  S. Georgia 43, 46
Poland 82, 113
polar bears 88
pollution 66–7, 116–18
ponies 127, 129
Ponting, Herbert 55, 101, 127
Port Lockroy 51, 135
Port Stanley 38, 42–3
Possession Islands 11
post 27, 80
prions 97–8
Protocol on Environmental
  Protection see Antarctic Treaty
psychological factors 83–4
Punta Arenas 18, 36

radios 80–81, 114
reindeer 45–6
research 61–70, 110, 116
reverse osmosis 74, 77
Ronne, Finn 137
Ronne Ice Shelf 137
Ross, Sir James Clark 55–6, 95,
  123–4
Ross Dependency 112
Ross Ice Shelf 55–6, 123
Ross Island 53–6, 53
  climate 22, 59
  see also McMurdo Station; Scott
  Base
Ross Sea 51–6, 52
Rothera Base 49, 59, 113
  shopping 30
Royds, Cape 53, 55
rubbish see waste
Russia (and former Soviet Union)
  30, 113, 114, 122, 138
  see also Vostok Station
Rymill, John 135

safety rules 30, 31, 73, 80–81, 83
  see also health

sailing to Antarctica 18
science see research
Scientific Committee on Antarctic
  Research (SCAR) 116
Scott, Captain Robert Falcon 125–8
  Discovery expedition 54, 126,
  129
  Terra Nova expedition ix, 54,
  56, 72, 126–8, 132, 133, 134
Scott Base (Ross Island) 53, 56, 112
  mail 27
  shopping 30
scuba-diving 5, 14, 30
  see also diving
scurvy 76
seabirds see birds
sea elephant see seals (elephant)
sea ice 67, 83
sealing:
  history 48, 65, 93, 122–3
  S. Georgia 44–6, 63
Sea Lion Island 42, 43
sea lions 41
seals 93–5, 103
  crabeater 95
  and dogs 78
  elephant 44–5, 50, 63, 94, 95
  fur seals 45, 63, 93, 103
  leopard 94–5
  research 63
  Ross 95
  on S. Georgia 44–5, 63, 95, 122
  Weddell 63, 88, 90, 93–4
  see also sealing; wildlife
sea-sickness 27
seasons 22–3, 59, 62
sea travel see ships
seawater see desalination
seaweed 102
seismology 69
self-catering, Falklands 43
Shackleton, Sir Ernest 129–31
  Imperial Transantarctic
  Expedition 53, 129–30, 133
  Nimrod expedition 53, 54, 129
shags 98
ships 18, 63, 80
  see also cruise ships
shopping 30–31
  equipment/clothing 24–5, 30–
  31
  S. Georgia 46
Signy Island 51, 60, 114

skidoos 78
skiing 17, 78
skuas 95–6, 103
sledges 78
sleeping bags 76
Smith, William 122
smoking 31, 118, 142
sno-cats 78–9
snow-blindness 27, 73
snow goggles see goggles
snowmobiles 78
snow petrels viii–ix, 97
socks 73
solar power 81
southern elephant seals see seals
southern lights 60
Southern Ocean 66, 108, 115
  biology 62–3, 64, 99
South Geomagnetic Pole 113, 114
South Georgia 17, 43–6, 45, 59
  climate 23
  history 44, 46, 100, 121,
  129–30, 135
  maps 28, 45
  see also wildlife
South Magnetic Pole 58, 129
South Orkney Islands 59, 125
South Pole:
  history 123, 125–32, 136–9
  research at 66, 67
  see also Geographic South Pole;
  South Geomagnetic
Pole; South Magnetic Pole; South
  Pole Station
South Pole (Amundsen-Scott)
  Station 59, 67, 74, 114, 118,
  137
South Sandwich Islands 28, 59
South Shetland Islands 18, 48–50,
  113, 122
  history 108, 122
souvenirs 30–31, 44, 46, 142
Soviet Union see Russia
sport 81
  see also Falklands; scuba–diving;
  swimming
springtails 102
squid 99
SSSIs 116, 142
stamps 27, 80
Stanley see Port Stanley
stations see bases
steamer duck 41

150   *Index: PER–STE*

Abercrombie and Kent Travel, Sloane Square House, Holbein Place, London SW1W 8NS, tel: 0171 730 9600, fax: 0171 730 9376. Expedition cruises to Antarctica, South Georgia and the Falkland Islands aboard Abercrombie and Kent's own ship *Explorer.*

Birdquest Ltd, Two Jays, Kemple End, Birdy Brow, Stonyhurst, Lancashire BB7 9QY, United Kingdom, tel: 01254 826116, fax: 01254 826780, email: ocean@birdquest.co.uk Group birdwatching tours to Antarctica, the Falklands and South Georgia.

Galapagos Adventure Tours, 37–39 Great Guildford Street, London SE1 0ES, tel: 0171 261 9890, fax: 0171 261 9890.

Journey Latin America, 16 Devonshire Road, Chiswick, London W4 2HD, tel: 0181 747 8315, fax: 0181 742 1312, Manchester 0161 832 1441, email: sales@journeylatinamerica.co.uk. Fully bonded ATOL 2828 ABTA V2522 AITO, Antarctic cruises from 12 days to 25 days, **Vessels:** *World Discoverer, Kapitan Khlebnikov, Professor Molchanov, Professor Khromov.* Unequalled range of scheduled flight connections from UK, including stopovers in the USA and Latin America.

Ocean Adventures Ltd, Two Jays, Kemple End, Stonyhurst, Lancashire BB7 9QY, United Kingdom, tel: 01254 826116, fax: 01254 826780, email: ocean@birdquest.co.uk Group birdwatching tours to Antarctica, the Falklands and South Georgia.

Ornitholidays,Worldwide Wildlife Tours, 1 Victoria Drive, Bognor Regis, West Sussex PO21 2PW, tel: 01243 821230, fax: 01243 829574.

Radisson Seven Seas Cruises, Quadrant House, 80–82 Regent Street, London W1R 6JB, tel: 0171 287 9060, fax: 0171 434 1410.

RADISSON SEVEN SEAS CRUISES

ADVENTURE SERIES

EXPERIENCE EARTH'S GREATEST ADVENTURES

*T*ravel in 5-star luxury to the most remote regions in the world. Experience nature in the most intimate circumstances — without impacting fragile ecosystems or sacrificing personal comfort, accompanied throughout by an experienced team of professional lecturers and guides.

The *m/s Hanseatic* and *m/s Bremen* are custom-designed ships created specifically for luxurious adventure cruising — a category of travel which they alone occupy. Carrying just 188 and 164 guests respectively, the *m/s Hanseatic* and *m/s Bremen* offer a degree of small-ship luxury and personal service not found on other adventure vessels.

COMPELLING DESTINATIONS

ANTARCTICA	NORTHWEST PASSAGE	ICELAND & GREENLAND
FALKLANDS & SOUTH GEORGIA	ALASKA & RUSSIAN FAR EAST	CHILEAN FJORDS AMAZON

- ⊕ 1A1 Super Ice Classification
- ⊕ Outstanding Crew to Guest Ratio
- ⊕ Fleet of Zodiac Landing Craft
- ⊕ Experienced Lecturers & Guides
- ⊕ Open Bridge Policy

- ⊕ Spacious ocean-view staterooms, measuring 190-475 sq. ft.
- ⊕ Single seating dining
- ⊕ Pre-cruise hotel night & economy airfare from the U.S. included
- ⊕ 10 to 20 night Cruise Adventures

For additional information, please contact
**Radisson Seven Seas Cruises in the U.S. at 1-800-285-1835
and in the U.K. at 0171-287-9060.**

m/s HANSEATIC   *m/s BREMEN*

U.S. - 600 CORPORATE DRIVE, SUITE 410, FORT LAUDERDALE, FL 33334
U.K. - 80-82 REGENT STREET, LONDON W1R 6JB ENGLAND   Ship's Bahamas

153